"Nancy Dunnan's expertise as a financial adviser is of inestimable value to women (as well as men). Her insights into the increasingly complicated realms of banking, savings, investments, insurance, long-term health care, retirement options, and many other areas are always full of wisdom. Nancy treats her readers with respect and talks with them as if they were trusted friends; she honors your intelligence and invites you to consider various strategies and options rather than lecturing or talking down to you. All of us benefit from her wise, thoughtful, and often entertaining counsel. Widows and friends of widows will find this book yet another Dunnan must-read."
—Rhode Ann Jones, director,
Bowdoin College Children's Center, Brunswick, Maine

"More than anyone I know, Nancy is the most qualified to cover the entire financial spectrum, from finding your checkbook and balancing it to collecting Social Security benefits and getting married again. Nancy's financial expertise and sensitivity will go a long way toward helping women get a financial grip at this difficult and important time in their lives."
—Anne Louise C. Van Nostrand, vice president,
Boston-based financial service organization

"There are a host of serious financial issues that widows, or those soon to be widowed, need to face. Nancy Dunnan's book identifies the priorities and provides the sound direction and wise answers every woman needs to know during this very difficult time. As an adviser, I find it invaluable."
—Edward J. Sullivan, managing director,
Bingham Legg Advisers LLC, Boston, Massachusetts

"Nancy Dunnan is supremely qualified to write on this critical and timely topic. A highly regarded expert in personal finance, saving, investing, and tax-wise strategies, she also very much understands and appreciates the special financial needs of women at transitional times in their lives."
  —Jane B. Kolson, director of Major Gifts,
  The Washington Opera, Washington, DC

"Nancy Dunnan talks finance from her heart. This talented author and adviser has helped millions of women take charge of their financial lives. Here she helps women going it alone plan for their financial futures. Smart, straight-talking, and positive, Nancy takes the reader by the wallet and walks her to financial security."
  —Ellen Pack, founder and senior vice president,
  Women.com

"Nancy Dunnan has always been *the* expert to trust for smart, clear, and comforting financial guidance. She educates without condescension and offers straightforward answers to sticky financial problems."
  —Linda Stern, *Newsweek*

"I can't imagine anyone I trust more than Nancy Dunnan with giving thoughtful, informed advice about handling money. In the many years she's been a guest on the show, she's always been astute and reliable. Our listeners have been so grateful for her recommendations. And in these times, her insights are all the more needed."
  —Melissa Eagan, producer, *The Leonard Lopate Show,*
  New York Public Radio (WNYC)

The
Widow's Financial Survival Guide

HANDLING
MONEY MATTERS
ON YOUR OWN

NANCY DUNNAN

A Perigee Book

P

A Perigee Book
Published by The Berkley Publishing Group
A division of Penguin Group (USA) Inc.
375 Hudson Street
New York, New York 10014

Copyright © 2003 by Nancy Dunnan
Text design by Tiffany Kukec
Cover design by Dorothy Wachtenheim

First edition: June 2003

Perigee trade paperback

ISBN: 0-399-52906-3

This book has been catalogued with the Library of Congress

Printed in the United States of America

10 9 8 7 6 5 4 3 2 1

*This book is dedicated to two of my favorite widows
who taught me so much about living life to its fullest . . .*

*Pauline Dodge Webel of Glen Head, New York, and Hobe Sound, Florida,
and Regina Ryan of New York City*

CONTENTS

Section Three:

Managing on Your Own

Section Four:

Investing and Estate Planning

ACKNOWLEDGMENTS

I wish to thank the following people for their expertise and guidance:

Robert Wilson, my creative literary agent

John Duff, my editor, whose wonderful common sense helped shape the manuscript

Marcy Ross, my editorial assistant

Jim Weikart of Weikart Tax Associates

Brian Herman, Attorney-at-Law

And to:

Linda Spiciarich, Evelyn Suzdak, Karl Witschonke, and George Woodward who made sure all the facts, phone numbers, websites, and addresses were correct.

INTRODUCTION

I don't expect you to find reading this book as much fun as you would find reading a novel or a play. But you simply *must* read it. It will enable you to take charge of your financial world and to make the right decisions as you forge ahead, handling life on your own.

You don't have to read it from beginning to end. You don't even have to read all of it. Simply pick and choose the chapters that apply to you.

You'll note that some financial and technical words are highlighted in *<u>italics and underlined</u>*. For each, there is a detailed definition in the Glossary at the end of the book. Understanding the terms used by pros in the business world will give you confidence and make it easier to ask intelligent questions and separate the right answers from the wrong answers.

In the end, this guide will not only make you financially smarter, it will also make you feel psychologically stronger and empowered. You will have accomplished what George Bernard Shaw wrote about in *Major Barbara*, where he paraphrases Euripides:

> *To stand from fear set free*
> *To breathe and wait*
> *To hold a hand uplifted over fate.*

That is what I want this book to do for you: set you free by enabling you to gain financial knowledge and with that knowledge to rise above what fate has presented.

Please know that although this book is not about bereavement, I fully realize that you are going through one of the, if not *the*, most stressful events of your life. But because my expertise is in the financial world and not in grief counseling, I am starting with the premise that your husband's funeral and burial have taken place and that you now are trying to make sense out of what happened. You know you must settle his estate, pay the bills, and make the money you have last as long as possible. Together we will go step by step down that path of financial independence and well-being.

I want you to begin by ordering a free copy of *The Consumer Action Handbook*. It is published every year by the Federal Information Center (800-688-9889). It covers many topics, including Social Security benefits, ways to save money, how to handle credit, protecting yourself from identity theft, health care issues, even how to repair, buy, lease, or rent a car. It also spells out how to complain and to whom you should address your complaints. It is an invaluable companion to the book you hold in your hands. You can also speak to a member of the well-trained staff, from 8:00 A.M. to 8:00 P.M., Monday through Friday, to get the best contact information to the appropriate government agencies.

The First Few Weeks

Chapter One

GETTING STARTED ON YOUR OWN

The best thing about the future is that it comes one day at a time.

—ABRAHAM LINCOLN

No one needs to tell you how devastating the death of your husband is. You already know. You are living through it. Widowed friends of mine tell me that at first they feel like curling up in a ball and letting someone else take over. They feel not only a great sense of loss and overwhelming sadness, but they also feel worried, even frightened about how they will manage financially. They feel unprepared to make decision after decision on their own.

That's why I wrote this book . . . to help you make the right choices, not only about how to save, invest, and handle credit but also about how to pay for your children's education, the remodeling of your house, or a vacation. You don't need to burden yourself by trying to get everything done at once. Nor do you need to do everything by yourself. But you do need to start to take charge and control of your financial world. Keep in mind that you're likely to live into your mid-80s or longer, so you want to be financially secure during those many years that lie ahead.

The Five Stages

After the funeral is over and your family and friends have returned to their lives, every widow is faced with a number of important tasks. You may have already taken care of some of them. Of those that remain, you may wish to take care of a number of them yourself. Others you may want a friend to help you with. And certain ones are best left to your lawyer.

Putting together your new financial life falls roughly into five time frames:

1. Immediate, day-to-day tasks, which will take up the first few weeks

2. Short-term financial matters, which will take one to three months

3. Short-term legal matters, which will take up to four months

4. Long-term tax issues, which can take up to a year, sometimes longer

5. Lifetime financial planning

Understanding these five stages and the fact that you cannot and must not resolve everything at once should give you a sense of relief. You do indeed have time to put the pieces of your life back together, albeit in a different fashion—to fly once again, but this time to fly solo. I will walk you through these five stages, but we will take them, as Lincoln advised, "one day at a time."

Ten Things You Need to Do Right Away

1. READ YOUR SPOUSE'S LETTER OF INSTRUCTION

If your husband left a *Letter of Instruction* telling you what to do in the event of his death, many aspects of settling his estate will be clear.

13 MUST-LOCATE PAPERS

Make up separate file folders for each of these documents, making as many copies as recommended in the detail discussion of each in this chapter.

1. Death certificate

2. Marriage certificate

3. Birth certificate

4. Social Security number

5. Will

6. Military discharge papers

7. Last income tax return

8. Power of attorney

9. Insurance policies

10. Car title

11. Retirement account records

12. Current bank, mutual fund, and brokerage account statements

13. Business partnership agreements

Although it is not a legal document, a Letter of Instruction spells out what the deceased wanted to take place. (Incidentally, you too should draw up your own Letter of Instruction.)

The letter should tell you where key personal and financial documents are located. If it does not or if there is no such letter, you will need to look through your husband's files, at home and/or at his office, in order to locate key papers required to settle the estate and to apply for the various benefits to which I hope you are entitled.

2. SET UP THE "ESTATE BOOK"

During this period, it is important to keep track of the many details related to settling your husband's estate. And, you'll be inundated with nonstop advice from family, friends, and your professional advisers. It's virtually impossible to remember all this information. I recommend you buy a special notebook or journal, designate it as the "Estate Book," and write down the names of everyone with whom you speak about business and legal matters, noting what they say and where they can be reached.

And, take care to record all expenses, including funeral costs, in the Estate Book. It's easy to lose track of details during these first difficult weeks.

3. PAY YOUR BILLS

This is a must. As difficult as it may be, get out your pile of unpaid bills and your checkbook. Don't wait until your husband's *estate* has been settled, as tempting as that may be. You'll simply wind up paying interest charges and late fees, be harassed by phone calls from bill collectors, and put blemishes on your <u>*credit report*</u> that will plague you for years to come.

Decide if you want to undertake the bill-paying task alone or with someone in your family. Then make space on your desk and put the bills in three categories: those you owe, those your husband owed and those you owe jointly. Total up each category as well as the grand total.

Begin by paying your bills. You want to keep your credit report pristine. Next pay as many as possible of the bills you and your husband owe jointly. Finally, do not pay your husband's bills; they should be taken care of by his estate, which we will discuss in Chapter 2.

> **$TIP: Look at each bill carefully to make sure that all the charges are legitimate. Scam artists prey on widows, using their credit cards, invading their checking accounts, and so on.**

> ## FOUR BILL-PAYING RULES TO KEEP IN MIND
>
> Paying bills is basically common sense, but if you're new to the task, you may not be aware of these four key rules.
>
> 1. Pay all bills on time to avoid late fees.
>
> 2. Pay the full amount to avoid finance charges.
>
> 3. If you can only make a partial payment, be sure to meet the minimum amount due.
>
> 4. When faced with several different credit card bills, make it your priority to pay off the one with the *highest interest rate first*, not the card with the highest dollar amount due.

Debt Doesn't Disappear You may not be able to pay all your bills immediately. That's not an unusual position; many widows find themselves in a cash crunch. But it's very important that you do not hide from the fact. It may be tempting to put your head in the sand, but debts, unlike rainy days, don't go away. Call each person or company you owe money to and tell them that your husband has died. Ask for an extension and together work out a payment plan.

Let them know you have yet to receive insurance proceeds or other widow's benefits. If you find making these phone calls too difficult, have a trusted family member, friend, attorney, or accountant make the calls for you.

If you are having problems with the bill from the funeral home, first call the director and ask for a written explanation of all charges. Funeral homes do not always make clear what all the costs are when you make burial arrangements. If you think the bill is unfair, contact:

- The Funeral Consumers Alliance in Hinesburg, VT (800-458-5563 or www.funerals.org). This nonprofit is active in consumer protection.

- The International Funeral Association in Reston, VA (800-645-7700 or www.icfa.org). The I.F.A. offers informal mediation of consumer complaints.

4. CALL YOUR HUSBAND'S EMPLOYER

Even though your husband's colleagues are aware of his death, you still need to officially notify the company in writing. If he worked for a large firm, send your letter to the human resources department; if he worked in a smaller organization, simply write to the president.

Your letter—typed, not handwritten—should include your husband's name (with his middle name or initial), his Social Security number, and the date he died. Enclose a copy of the death certificate. Include your phone and fax numbers and, if you wish, your email address.

This is also a good time to ask for a list of spousal benefits. These could include insurance, _vested benefits_, a 401(k) plan, a stock option plan, a stock purchase plan, supplemental insurance, medical benefits, and unused vacation or sick leave pay. If your husband was disabled, you also may be entitled to widow's disability benefits.

> **$TIP:** If you were covered by your husband's medical plan at work, find out if you and your children will automatically be covered. If not, apply for continuation of coverage under the federal _COBRA_ plan. You must apply within 60 days of death and although you will have to pay the premiums, they are likely to be far less than if you take out individual coverage. (See Chapter 8 for details.)

5. STOP MAKING PAYMENTS

Make a list of activities in which your husband was involved as well as services he subscribed to that no longer need to be maintained. (Of course, you may wish to keep some or all of the joint accounts and memberships you held together.) Call or write those you plan to discontinue, stating that you will be ending payment, mentioning your husband's date of death. It's easy to forget about such things, but this list will jog your memory:

- Bank accounts
- Cell phone and answering service
- Club memberships: athletic/ health, automobile, book, collegiate, community, religious, and social
- Course or class tuition
- Credit and affinity cards
- Credit union accounts
- Debit cards
- Educational courses
- Email account
- Newspaper, magazine, and newsletter subscriptions
- Pager service
- Personal service contracts: trainers, coaches, and so on

6. CONTINUE TO MAKE PAYMENTS

Although you have already sorted out bills to be paid, depending upon the time of the month when you did so, you may not have run across these must-be-paid bills:

- Automatic payments (arrange with bank or credit card companies)
- Automobile payments
- Child's college tuition
- Debt consolidation loans
- Home equity loan
- Mortgage or rent
- Property taxes
- Student loans
- Utility bills

7. GATHER KEY PAPERS

The following are the key documents that you will need to locate and have on hand:

Your Husband's Death Certificate You will need more copies of the death certificate than you can imagine. I recommend getting at least ten copies or up to 20 if your husband had many different savings and investment accounts. Most companies insist on having a certificate to close out an account.

You will also need a death certificate to apply for retirement and pension plan survivor's benefits; to file for each life insurance, Social Security, and veteran's benefits claim; to gain access to accounts at banks, brokerage firms, and mutual fund companies; and to transfer the title on real estate and the ownership of stocks and bonds.

The funeral director will order as many certified copies as you need. Over order. It's much easier to get them now. If you need more a year from now, you may have to go to your state's vital statistics agency or county health department, where you'll be certain to encounter miles of red tape.

> **$TIP: Most companies insist upon a certified death certificate, which has a raised seal. However, ask first. You will save money if you can use a photocopy of a certified certificate.**

Marriage Certificate If your marriage certificate was not in your safe deposit box, get a copy from the county clerk where the marriage license was issued.

Birth Certificate If your husband's birth certificate was not in your safe deposit box, you can get it from the state or county public records office where he was born.

> **$TIP: The National Center for Health Statistics in Hyattsville, MD (301-458-4636 or www.cdc.gov/nchs/), has information on how to find records in various states. On the website's home page, click on "Help Obtaining Birth, Death, Marriage or Divorce Certificates."**

Your Husband's Most Recent Will If the original was not in your safe deposit box or in your husband's personal files, the lawyer who drew up the will may have it in his office.

Military Discharge Papers If you did not find a copy of your husband's discharge papers, request a copy from:

National Personnel Records Center
9700 Page Boulevard
St. Louis, MO 63132-5200

On the envelope, note the branch of service: Army, Navy, Coast Guard, or Marines.

Recent Income Tax Return This should be among his papers or with your accountant. If you cannot locate copies in either place, you must fill out IRS Form 4506, "Request for Copy of Transcript of Tax Form." To get a copy of Form 4506, log on to www.irs.gov and type the number in the "Search Forms" box, or call 800-829-3676. There is a $23 fee for each tax period requested.

8. VISIT YOUR SAFE DEPOSIT BOX

If you have a jointly owned safe deposit box, set aside a morning to go to your bank. In addition to the box key, take along a notepad, pen or pencil, and a briefcase or tote bag that can be securely closed and fastened.

Once the bank officer delivers your box, take it into one of the private rooms. *Make a list of everything in the box.* Then put the following items into your briefcase or bag to take home if they are in the box:

- Your husband's will
- Insurance policies
- Military discharge papers
- Family birth certificates
- Retirement documents
- Marriage license
- Real estate deeds and leases

- Buy-sell agreements for your husband's business
- Stock and bond certificates

Make two photocopies of all these documents, either at the bank, your office, or a stationery store. Leave one set with your attorney. Then, when you arrive home, put the originals and copies in a file labeled "Safe Deposit Box." And, add the list of all items that remain at the bank to the file.

13 THINGS YOU DON'T NEED TO DO RIGHT NOW

Until you are able to make unemotional decisions, don't:

1. Sell your house
2. Sell your stocks, bonds, or mutual funds
3. Make any financial decisions that can't be reversed
4. Buy a new car
5. Buy life insurance
6. Upgrade your apartment or house
7. Go on a spending spree
8. Borrow money
9. Lend money
10. Give away money
11. Let children or other relatives make your money decisions
12. Give out your numbers—Social Security, credit card, or driver's license
13. Talk with strangers

$TIP: In some states, even when two people have access to a box, the box is sealed when one of the owners dies. If you face this situation, ask your lawyer to get the court's permission for you to open the box.

9. CONTACT YOUR HUSBAND'S CREDITORS

Request that their bills be sent to the executor of the estate. (See Chapter 2 for details.)

10. CHANGE YOUR BENEFICIARIES

If your husband was the beneficiary of your insurance policy or retirement account, you will need to name someone else. You should also update your will. (See Chapter 11 for details.)

Bottom Line

You've just taken your first steps toward a new life. And, as difficult as it may have been, keep in mind the words of Hal Borland, "No winter lasts forever, no spring skips its turn."

Chapter Two

SETTLING YOUR HUSBAND'S ESTATE

Don't be afraid to take a big step when one is indicated.
You can't cross a chasm in two small jumps.
— DAVID LLOYD GEORGE

When your husband died, all of his assets, including physical possessions and finances, became part of his estate. What happens to his assets is supervised by the state's probate court. (In certain states it is known as surrogate's court or the chancery court.)

The task of <u>settling the estate</u> may at first seem like a daunting one, a very big step. Perhaps it conjures up visions of expensive lawyers, squabbling families, and reams of paperwork. But don't let it frighten you. In most cases it is generally not so much an overwhelming process as it is a time-consuming one. It can take months, in some cases even years, to complete, depending upon the value of the estate and the number of beneficiaries. We'll go through the process step by step, so you will know what takes place at each juncture.

Keep in mind that in most states you are entitled to a portion of your husband's assets—even if you are not named in the will. If you are not included in the will, you must hire a very experienced probate attorney. Do not try to handle it alone. The attorney may have you file an "election against the will by the surviving spouse" to make certain that you receive some part of the estate if you have been left less than the amount prescribed by your state's statute.

All About Probate

The legal process through which ownership and title of your husband's assets are transferred to his heirs is known as *probate*. At the beginning of probate, his will is reviewed by the court to make certain it is indeed his will and that it is legally valid. The will at this point is a public document and can be read by anyone.

Next, your attorney or the *executor* (explained below) will notify all the beneficiaries named in the will by mail. Each will receive a copy of the will. Your husband's creditors will also be notified so they can let the court know about any outstanding debts.

The probate process is not free. Fees vary from state to state and usually are based on the fair market value of the assets in the estate.

Probate is necessary if any one of the following conditions apply:

- There is an *asset* titled in your husband's name only.

- The *beneficiary* of your husband's life insurance policy or annuity is listed as "estate" rather than a person's name.

- The primary beneficiary of your husband's life insurance policy or annuity has died and your husband has not named a backup or secondary beneficiary.

- The secondary beneficiary of any of these policies has died.

Let's look at a theoretical example. You and your husband own your house together in *tenancy by the entirety*. You both have IRAs in which you name each other as beneficiaries. He has a 401(k) and has named you as beneficiary. You have a jointly owned brokerage account, and your husband owned a hundred shares of IBM. Only one asset is required to go through probate: the hundred shares of IBM. The rest of the estate would pass outside probate and go directly to you.

ROLE OF THE EXECUTOR

The executor's duties are to probate the will. That is, the executor makes sure that the debts of the deceased are paid and that his remaining property is given to the rightful owners. Probate operates according to state, not federal, laws.

If your husband had a will, he most likely named an executor. That person may be you—in which case the correct term is executrix—or it may be someone else—perhaps an adult child, close relative, or friend. Some people choose a lawyer, accountant, or financial consultant because of that person's expertise. An institution can also be named executor. One can serve as executor and also be a beneficiary of a will.

IF THERE IS NO WILL OR NO EXECUTOR

If your husband died without a will, which is to die _intestate_, or if he did not name an executor in his will, you will most likely be appointed as the administrator of the estate, or the personal representative (P.R.). Although you do not have to accept this appointment, I encourage you to do so as it will speed up the process.

The laws governing this situation, which vary from state to state, are called intestacy laws. They provide directions for dividing the estate among survivors.

BONDING

The executor or personal representative of the estate must be _bonded_ for an amount that is equal to the value of the estate's property plus any annual income that the estate earns. The court determines the amount of the bond, and the estate usually pays the premium. In some cases the bonding requirement is waived by the will or the court will allow a reduced bond, especially if the estate's representative is also the principal beneficiary.

The Probate Process: In Court and Out

The following information assumes that you are either the executrix or P.R.

To make it easy to understand, I've broken down the executor and the probate process into nine basic steps, through which your lawyer will guide you:

Step 1. Locating the will. This first step involves not just locating your husband's will, but the last will written plus any amendments (known as *codicils*).

Step 2. Initiating the probate process. After locating the will, your next step is to fill out an official form, which your lawyer will obtain, and then appear in probate court (in the county or city where your husband lived at the time of death) with the original will and a certified death certificate.

If for some reason the will is found invalid, the court will order that the creditors and taxes be paid. The remainder of the estate will be distributed in accordance with state law.

Step 3. Informing affected parties. Upon verification that the will is valid, you then must write letters and publish notices in newspapers informing potential heirs and creditors that the probate process is moving ahead. After filing such notices, creditors, heirs, and others can file claims against the estate. (Your attorney can take care of this for you.)

A BIT OF PERSONAL ADVICE

Do not rush into probate immediately after your husband's death. In most states, you can wait a month or so to start the process and by then you may feel better able to handle the situation and more comfortable with the decision making involved.

Having said that, I want to also urge you not to put it off too long. Assets held in your husband's name alone cannot be transferred to your name without probate. Nor will you be able to sell them.

Step 4. Filing an inventory and appraisal. You must draw up a complete list of the estate's assets, including all real estate, personal property, and financial holdings, and you must appraise their value. When compiling the inventory, a distinction must be made between the property that your husband owned individually and that owned jointly with the right of survivorship. (See Executrix's Checklist and Inventory Checklist, on pages 22 and 23.)

Step 5. Opening a checking account. The checking account for the estate is used to pay costs related to the probate process. (*Caution:* Never use your personal account.) In order to set up this account, you will need a taxpayer identification number for the estate. This involves filling out IRS Form SS-4, available by calling 800-329-3676 or by going online at: www.irs.gov.

> **$TIP:** You may receive checks made out to your husband from those who are unaware of his death. As executor, you may endorse them and deposit them into the estate's account. Again, do not use your personal account.

Step 6. Paying creditors, taxes, and fees. The next step is to pay all debts and taxes owed by the estate. Taxes could include personal income tax, estate income tax, inheritance tax, estate tax, and credit estate tax. There will also be court fees, the cost of the executor's bond, and his or her administrative expenses.

Step 7. Drawing up a final accounting. This cannot be done until the inventory appraisal has been completed and outstanding debts and taxes have been paid. This final balance sheet shows the value of the estate, any income or interest earned, debts paid, money owed, and tax payments.

Step 8. Distributing the assets. The penultimate step is to distribute all assets to beneficiaries as specified in the will.

Step 9. Closing the estate. After the accounting has been approved and all assets distributed, the estate is officially closed by submitting a sworn statement to the court. This paper shows evidence, such as signed receipts, that assets were distributed to the beneficiaries.

Whoever the executor or executrix, he or she is legally obligated to act in the interest of the deceased and follow his wishes as spelled out in the will. That sometimes means defending the terms of the will against arguments by heirs or others.

If all of this seems like more than you want to handle, you can hire an attorney to help with the probate process and an accountant to take care of the taxes. Their fees are chargeable to the estate as expenses of administration.

> **$TIP:** If for some reason you do not wish to be the executor or are unable to (perhaps due to health reasons or extensive travel), you need to file a declination with the court. Then, the contingent executor will take over the position. If your husband did not name a contingent executor, the court will appoint one.

The Executor's Fee and Expenses

Generally, the estate is responsible for paying the executor a fee. The fee, which may be mentioned in the will or determined by state law, can be waived if you so wish. (*Note:* If the executor is an attorney, in most states he or she cannot collect both an executor's fee and an attorney's fee for the same estate.)

Executors are generally reimbursed from the estate for reasonable expenses, such as travel.

Finally, keep a copy of all records pertaining to the settling of the estate for several years.

Nonprobate Assets

You do not need to report nonprobate assets to the court. Nonprobate assets pass to survivors outside the will and are not subject to claims made by your husband's creditors, with the exception of federal and state death taxes. In some cases, an entire estate is nonprobate. Below is a typical list of nonprobate assets:

- Life Insurance Proceeds
- Property owned by you and your husband in *joint tenancy with right of survivorship* (JTWRS)
- Property owned by you and your husband in tenancy by the entirety
- Property held by an inter vivas trust
- Retirement plan benefits in which there are named beneficiaries. These include IRAs, 401(k)s, and pension plans. (Exception: If the estate was named as beneficiary or if the beneficiary has died.)
- Savings bonds owned jointly by you and your husband
- Sick leave not taken by your husband prior to his death
- *Totten trusts*, or joint bank accounts set up by you and your husband with you as the beneficiary
- *Transfer on death accounts*, set up by you and your husband with a mutual fund company
- Vacation pay earned by your husband but not paid to him prior to his death
- Wages earned by your husband but not paid to him prior to his death

(*Caution:* There are some exceptions in some states regarding nonprobate assets.)

$TIP: Your state may allow motor vehicles below a certain dollar value and owned in your husband's name only to be transferred directly to you or other beneficiaries.

For More Help

About Being an Executor, Life Advice (800-MET-LIFE or www. lifeadvice.com)

How to Administer an Estate: A Step-by-Step Guide for Families and Friends, by Stephen G. Christianson (Citadel Press, 4th ed., 2001)

Bottom Line

By settling your husband's estate, you have made enormous progress, something Ralph Waldo Emerson defined as "the activity of today (which leads to) the assurance of tomorrow."

THE EXECUTRIX'S CHECKLIST

☐ Locate the will

☐ Hire or at least consult with an attorney

☐ Apply to appear before the probate court

☐ Notify beneficiaries who are named in the will

☐ Set up publication of a notice to all creditors

☐ Mail a notice to each creditor

☐ Send notices of your husband's death to the post office, utilities, and bank companies and credit card issuers

☐ Make an inventory of all assets

☐ Have appropriate assets appraised

☐ Collect debts owed to the estate

☐ Contact your husband's employer regarding unpaid salary, insurance, and other employee benefits

☐ File for Social Security, veterans, and private sector benefits

☐ File for life insurance and other benefits

☐ File city, state, and/or federal tax returns

☐ File state death and federal estate tax returns

☐ Pay legitimate claims against the estate

☐ Distribute assets to beneficiaries

☐ Obtain signed receipts from beneficiaries

☐ File papers to finalize the estate

INVENTORY FILING CHECKLIST

You will require the following to file the inventory:

☐ Your husband's will

☐ A list of the contents of the safe deposit box

☐ A list of all savings, checking, brokerage, and money market accounts

☐ A list of all stocks, bonds, bank CDs, and mutual funds

☐ A list of all real estate, solely owned or with a business partner

☐ A list of all corporations he owned, including partial ownership

☐ A list of all partnerships, limited or otherwise

☐ A copy of all insurance policies (life, disability, health, automobile, umbrella, property, casualty, and so on)

☐ A list of IRAs, 401(k)s, and pension plans and retirement accounts

☐ A list of funeral expenses

☐ A copy of all trusts

☐ A list of all debts and claims against the estate

☐ Copies of the last three or five years' tax returns

Section Two

Claiming All That's Yours

Chapter Three

MONEY FROM THE GOVERNMENT

Government exists to protect freedom and enlarge the opportunities of every citizen.

—LYNDON BAINES JOHNSON

You're now ready to take your next step and that is to enlarge your opportunities and those of your children by collecting benefits from the government. I urge you to apply for every remotely possible benefit. It is better to be turned down than not to apply at all and miss out.

Social Security Benefits

If your husband's Social Security benefits were being paid via direct deposit, call or write the bank or other financial institution that was receiving them. Your letter should include your husband's name, Social Security number, address, and date and place of death.

If the benefits were being paid by check and you continue to receive them in the mail, do *not* cash any checks for the month in which your husband died. Return them to Social Security.

WHAT YOU MAY RECEIVE

If your husband worked at least 40 quarters before he died, you are entitled to what are called "survivor's benefits." In order to collect them, you'll need to notify the Social Security Administration (800-772-1213; or, for the hearing impaired, 800-325-0778). Call between 7:00 A.M. and 7:00 P.M., ET, Monday through Friday. Do so promptly because, in some cases, benefits are not retroactive. To read online what the government says about this, go to www.ssa.gov/pubs/10084.html.

There are two types of possible benefits:

1. **The $225 death benefit** for burial expenses: In order to receive this check, you must complete the appropriate form, which you can get at your local Social Security office. Or, if you prefer, the funeral director can complete the form and then apply the $225 directly to the cost of your husband's funeral.

2. **The survivor's benefit** varies depending upon your age and your husband's work. Because the rules are fairly complex, I urge you to make an appointment with your local Social Security office. Take along the following:

- Your own birth certificate
- You and your husband's marriage certificate
- You and your husband's Social Security numbers
- Your husband's death certificate
- A copy of your husband's most recent federal income tax return
- A copy of your husband's W-2 form for the last year of work before his death
- The name of your bank and your account number for direct deposit

If you are applying for your children's benefits, you will need their birth certificates and Social Security numbers as well.

You may be entitled to benefits if any one of these applies:

- You are 60 or older
- You are 50 or older and disabled
- You are under 60 and are taking care of dependent children (under age 16) or disabled children of any age

- His surviving child is up to age 18
- His surviving child is between the ages 18 and 19 and in school full time (In most cases the student must be in elementary or high school; college-age students rarely qualify.)
- His surviving child is over 18 but became disabled before age 22

$TIP: There are two little-known rules that provide additional benefits. One or the other may apply to you in the future:

1. Your children's benefits will not end should you remarry, even if their stepfather adopts them and/or helps with their support. Your children's benefits come to an end only when they marry or reach age 18.

2. When your youngest surviving child reaches age 16, your benefits stop. However, make sure you restart them again when you turn 60 or, if you're disabled, when you reach 50.

HOW MUCH?

Widow's benefits typically range from 71.5% of the deceased husband's benefit amount (starting at age 60) up to 100% of the amount your husband would be receiving if he were alive (starting at age 65). If you are disabled, you can collect 71.5% beginning at age 50.

Note: Starting in 2005, the age at which the 100% is payable will be increased gradually until it reaches age 67 in 2029.

$TIP: If both you and your husband were receiving Social Security benefits before he died, you are entitled to the greater of the two benefits. For example, if you're entitled to $600 a month on your own record and $500 a month as a widow, you will receive $600 per month, not $1,100.

THE OFF-SET RULE

If you worked at a job not covered by Social Security—usually in a government agency—and you're entitled to a pension from that job in addition to a widow's benefit from Social Security, the amount you receive will probably be based on the so-called "off-set" rule: two-thirds of the government pension will be deducted from your Social Security widow's benefits.

If, for example, you are eligible for $500 a month from Social Security as a widow and $600 a month from your pension, two-thirds of that pension ($400) will be deducted from your widow's benefit, leaving you with just $100 from Social Security.

There are two exceptions to the off-set rule. Be sure to ask the person you speak with at Social Security about both:

1. If your pension is from government work but you paid Social Security taxes at the end of your career, your Social Security benefit would not be reduced.

2. If your spouse qualified for both a government pension and a Social Security benefit, you'd be entitled to receive a widow's benefit in each case.

For More Help

The Social Security Administration (SSA) has two helpful booklets you should read, just to make certain you are not overlooking anything that is your due. They are available by phone at 800-772-1213 or online at www.ssa.gov.

Survivors Benefits, Publication #05-10084

Social Security: Understanding the Benefits, Publication #05-10024

Veteran's Benefits

If your husband was a veteran, you may be entitled to several different benefits, including a burial stipend and insurance proceeds.

BURIAL ALLOWANCE

This allowance is offered to widows who paid for a veteran's burial or funeral and . . .

- Have not been reimbursed by another government agency or other sources
- Whose husbands were discharged under conditions other than dishonorable

In addition, at least one of the following conditions must be met:

- Your husband died because of a service-related disability
- Your husband was receiving a VA pension or compensation at the time of death
- Your husband died in a VA hospital or while in a nursing home under a VA contract

HOW MUCH?

If your husband's death was service-related, the VA will pay $2,000. If he is buried in a VA national cemetery, some or all of the cost of moving the deceased from the funeral home to the cemetery may be reimbursed.

If your husband's death was not service-related, the VA will pay up to $300 toward burial and funeral expenses and $300 for plot interment allowance. If the death happened while your husband was in a VA hospital or at a nursing home under contract with the VA, some or all of the costs for transporting his body may be reimbursed.

You must fill out VA Form 21-530, "Application for Burial Allowance." You will need to include proof of the veteran's military service (Form DD 214), certified death and marriage certificates, Social Security numbers, and copies of all funeral and burial bills you have paid. Mail the form and documents to the nearest VA regional office. For a list, call 800-827-1000 or log on to www.va.gov.

Note: The VA does not keep service records. The National Personnel Records Center (NPRC) keeps them, which is under the jurisdiction of the U.S. National Archives Records Administration (NARA). The address is:

700 Pennsylvania Avenue, NW
Washington, DC 20408
(86-NARA-NARA or www.archives.gov/facilities)

You will need to complete Standard Form 180, "Request Pertaining to Military Records," and mail it to yet a different place:

National Personnel Records Center
Military Personnel Records
9700 Page Avenue
St. Louis, MO 63132

VETERAN'S LIFE INSURANCE

The VA has a number of life insurance programs, some in place for those who served prior to 1965 and others for those who were on active duty or became disabled. If your husband owned a VA life insurance policy, call the nearest VA office to make a claim.

VETERAN'S EDUCATIONAL ASSISTANCE FOR DEPENDENTS

If your husband's death was service-related, or if when he died he was completely disabled due to service-related causes, you are entitled not only to the burial allowance but also to a monthly allowance to help educate you or your children. Payments for children often last up until age 26 and do not end if they marry.

There are a number of other assistance programs for surviving spouses and children. Set aside time to go over them via phone with a benefits officer at the nearest VA office. You'll find the VA staff especially courteous and kind.

For More Help

The Department of Veterans Affairs has at least one regional office in each state, plus offices in Puerto Rico and the Philippines. You can find your nearest VA benefits office by calling 800-827-1000.

Federal Benefits for Veterans and Dependents is available online or by writing to:

> Office of Public Affairs
> Department of Veterans Affairs
> 810 Vermont Avenue NW
> Washington, DC 20420

The Veterans of Foreign Wars (www.vfw.org/news/state.shtml) has a list of contacts for state veterans benefits.

Bottom Line

Goethe defined government as "that which teaches us to govern ourselves." Now that you have collected your due from the government, you have increased your options for governing your own life.

Chapter Four

MONEY FROM THE PRIVATE SECTOR

Never give up and never give in.
—Hubert H. Humphrey

For some reason, Americans seem to have an easier time going after the government for benefits—such as those provided by Social Security—than they do taking on the corporate world. Don't allow yourself to fall into this reluctant group. Instead follow Hubert Humphrey's advice and go after every conceivable benefit. They are *not* handouts. Believe me, they will arrive in your mailbox only if you're legally entitled to them. And, keep in mind that these benefits were either paid for by your husband or offered to him as part of a work package. They are your entitlement and a very minor compensation for the fact he is no longer with you.

Life Insurance Claims

We'll start here because chances are your husband had an individual or group policy. Unfortunately, the proceeds from his policy won't come to you; you must go after them. That means you must file a *claim*. And, of course, the sooner you apply, the sooner you'll receive the money and be able to invest it or use it to cover expenses and pay bills.

FINDING THE POLICY

In Chapter 1, we listed insurance policies as one of those must-find papers. There are two types to look for: a policy provided by your husband's employer and a policy that your husband (or the two of you together) purchased on your own. Perhaps you've already located a policy in your husband's files or in your safe deposit box. If so, you can skip this section and go to the section, "Getting in Touch with the Insurance Company," which follows in the chapter.

AN INDIVIDUALLY PURCHASED POLICY

If you haven't found an actual policy and you have an insurance agent, phone him. He will send you the appropriate forms to fill out in order to claim benefits.

If you don't have an agent, go through all checkbook registers and write down the names of any insurance companies to which _premiums_ were sent. (See page 40 for the names of some of the larger companies.) If you come upon a company name that is unfamiliar, check to see if it is listed with either of these insurance directories: A. M. Best (908-439-2200 or www.ambest.com) or Abbycon Special Directories (www.abbycon.com).

> $TIP: While running through the check register, jot down in your Estate Book the names of any financial and mutual companies, brokerage firms, credit unions, and banks you come upon. We'll come back to those later on.

A GROUP POLICY

In addition to an individually owned policy, your husband might have had a group policy issued by his employer or through a religious, business, or professional association. Group coverage is also offered through fraternal associations, such as the Elks, Kiwanis, Knights of Columbus, Lions, or Moose.

OTHER TYPES OF POLICIES

Automobile insurance may pay a death benefit if your husband was killed because of an auto collision. Cancer care policies pay a death benefit if the insured died of cancer. Credit life policies pay off the outstanding balance owed on installment debt. Mortgage life insurance pays off the mortgage. Travel accident policies, issued by automobile associations and gasoline credit card companies, offer some benefits. Credit cards may pay a death benefit. Lastly, worker's compensation pays out if your husband's death was work-related.

> **$TIP: If in the course of going through the checkbook you find that premiums were paid automatically after your husband died, you can ask that they be reimbursed.**

GETTING IN TOUCH WITH THE INSURANCE COMPANY

The next step is preparing a written claim letter. It must include the policy number, the actual policy (or the completed "lost policy" form), a certified copy of your husband's death certificate, his Social Security number, and your Social Security number.

If there is more than one beneficiary, each beneficiary must file a claim form. If the first beneficiary named on the policy has died, a certified copy of that person's death certificate will be required. If a trustee was named as beneficiary, then the trustee files the claim form.

Once you submit the form, the company will determine if there is any reason not to pay the claim. The two most likely reasons for denial are suicide and knowingly having cancer when the policy was issued and not informing the insurance company of the fact.

You can expect the process to take ten to fourteen working days, sometimes longer. If you have a financial emergency, many companies will advance up to $10,000 to you as beneficiary. You can review the procedure with the company.

GETTING PAID

You will probably be given one of three general types of payouts, although there are quite a few other options:

1. A lump-sum payment in which you receive the full death benefit all at once

2. An interest-bearing checking account in your name

3. An annuity

Regardless of the option, life insurance proceeds, when paid to a named beneficiary, are not regarded as taxable income at the federal or state level.

An _annuity_ is the most complicated of the three. With an annuity you could:

1. Receive monthly payments over your lifetime with payments stopping when you die—called a non-refund life annuity

2. Receive payments for a specific number of years (5, 10, 15, 20, even 25) whether you live or die, but there are no payments after the specified time period—called period certain only annuity

3. Receive payments for a specific number of years (5, 10, 15, or 20) whether you live or die but if you live longer than the guaranteed period time, payments still continue—called life annuity with guaranteed, time-specified payments

4. Receive period payments for life with any unused money in the policy going to someone you designate—called installment refund

With the majority of policies, once you make a decision, that's it. You cannot change it. There are some policies, however, that allow you to change the payout option once, within a 60-day window of opportunity after the first benefit payout.

Unless your attorney or accountant advises you otherwise, a lump-sum payment generally makes the most sense for most women.

Because this is a period of transition in your life, put the money in a federally insured bank CD or a money market fund. This is not the time to be investing in the stock market, unless you are extremely experienced and successful at doing so.

Annuity Claims

If your husband had an annuity, the claims procedure is the same as with an insurance policy. The terms of the annuity will determine if you receive benefits in a lump sum or in ongoing payments. Your accountant will explain the tax situation. There are a wide variety of annuities. I want you to be aware of the four most common:

1. Single premium deferred annuity. The interest rate for this lump-sum type annuity is guaranteed for a specific time. Once the time period is over, a new rate is guaranteed for a new time period.

2. Variable annuity. The value of the annuity or the principal, whichever is greater, is guaranteed to the beneficiary.

3. Tax sheltered annuity. Known as a TSA, this annuity is offered to school employees and county and municipal workers. A TSA may have a fixed or variable yield.

4. Indexed annuity. This type has a minimum guaranteed interest rate but will earn more if the index it is tied to, such as the Standard & Poor 500 Index, performs well.

Employment Benefits

As we mentioned in Chapter 1, if your husband was still working when he died, you need to contact his employer. You may be entitled to a number of benefits.

The information you receive may be complicated or confusing. Don't be shy about not understanding all the legalese and don't think you're bothering the benefits administrator when asking for explanations. This is your entitlement, not theirs. Your financial future should be the focus of your energy, not being nice.

Here are the possible benefits the company may owe you:

1. Health Insurance. Under COBRA, you and your children are entitled to keep your medical benefits under your husband's plan for 18 months (sometimes longer) following his death. You will have to pay the premiums, but they will be at the group rate.

2. Pension and Retirement Plans. Your husband may have participated in a *401(k) plan*, *403(b) plan*, or *457 plan*; or a thrift savings plan, a *profit sharing plan*, a stock option plan, or a stock purchase plan.

3. Life insurance. You may be entitled to money if your husband's employer offered employees life insurance.

4. Unpaid money. Two sources of money that are often overlooked are accrued but unpaid bonuses and accrued but unpaid vacation time.

FINDING A COMPANY THAT MOVED OR WENT OUT OF BUSINESS

If your husband had a pension with a company that is no longer in business, or if he worked for a number of companies over the years, you will need to do a little detective work to find all possible benefits. Begin by contacting:

The Pension Benefit Guaranty Corporation
1200 K Street, NW
Washington, DC 20005
800-400-7242 or www.pbgc.gov

This federal agency protects private defined benefit pension plans—the type that promise to pay a specific monthly benefit upon retirement and to widows. This group will help you track down a pension plan. It does not, however, cover 401(k) or 403(b) plans.

14 LEADING LIFE INSURANCE COMPANIES

Aetna: Call local agent or www.aetna.com

Allstate: Call local agent or www.allstate.com

American General: 800-528-2011 or www.americangeneral.com

Chubb: 908-903-2000 or www.chubb.com

CNA: 312-822-5000 or www.cna.com

Equitable: 888-855-5100 or www.equitable.com

Farmers: 208-239-8400 or www.farmers.com

Hartford: 800-833-5575 or www.thehartford.com

Lafayette: 765-477-7411 or www.llic.com

Mutual of Omaha: 800-775-6000 or www.mutualofomaha.com

Nationwide: Call local agent or www.nationwide.com

Northwestern Mutual: 414-271-1444 or
http://ww2.northwesternmutual.com

SAFECO: Call local agent or www.safeco.com

State Farm: Call local agent or www.statefarm.com

If your husband worked for a publicly traded company that moved but you don't know where, get a copy of the company's annual report; it will have the current address. Or retrieve the address from the company's website. Go to www.google.com and type in the company's name.

If the company was not publicly traded, check with the local chamber of commerce where it was headquartered or had offices. The chamber may know where the firm moved. Other possible sources of information include the labor union if the company employed union members, your husband's old coworkers, and the office of unclaimed property in the capital of the state where you think a company was located.

Finally, try the National Association of Unclaimed Property Administrators (www.unclaimed.org). This is an excellent source for all kinds of lost funds, including stocks, bonds, bank accounts, utility deposits, and more. Or contact your state treasurer or state comptroller's office, which administers the unclaimed funds program for that state. The number will be listed in the government pages of the phone book.

USING AN IRA ROLLOVER

If you will be receiving a lump-sum distribution from a qualified retirement plan, you have the option of transferring the money directly from the *custodian* of your husband's retirement plan to the custodian of your IRA. Called an *IRA rollover*, this enables you to avoid paying a 20% withholding tax on the amount of the lump-sum distribution.

Two cautions:

1. You will be told that you can also take the money via a check, in which case you have 60 days in which to place the money in your own IRA. Don't do this. You may be tempted to spend some or all of it. Or, you may lose track of the 60-day window of opportunity. In both cases, you'll be hit with a tax bill, so instead use the IRA-to-IRA rollover method.

2. The tax implications of retirement payouts are complex and confusing. After you know what benefits you're entitled to, discuss them with your accountant. Together, decide what option is best for you.

IF THE ANSWER IS "NO BENEFITS"

Don't simply say okay. It may not be okay. Retirement plans and benefits are fraught with problems—oversights, fraud, typos, and honest mistakes. If you believe you are entitled to survivor benefits, ask the company to send you the "Summary Plan Description" and a copy of the latest "Participant Statement." If you find supporting evidence that you are being misled, contact your attorney. Ask if he or she has experience in the area of retirement benefits; if not, ask for a recommendation.

Sample Claims Letter to an Insurance Company
With Policy Information

Your name
Your street address
Your city, state, and zip code

Your telephone/fax numbers

Date

Insurance company name
Their street address
Their city, state, and zip code

re: Your husband's name
Policy #00000

Dear Claims Agent:

This is to notify you that my husband, (husband's name), died on (date) in (city), (state).

His Social Security number was _____.

I wish to apply for the insurance benefits provided by this policy. Please send me the necessary forms along with instructions for applying for benefits.

Sincerely yours,
Signature
Name typed/printed

Sample Claims Letter to an Insurance Company
Without Policy Information

Your name
Your street address
Your city, state, and zip code

Your telephone/fax numbers

Date

Insurance company name
Their street address
Their city, state, and zip code

re: Your husband's name

Dear Claims Agent:

This is to notify you that my husband, (husband's name), died on (date) in (city), (state).

His Social Security number was _____.

It is my understanding that your company issued a life insurance policy insuring the life of my husband, (husband's name). I have not been able to locate the policy itself.

Please let me know if a policy is in effect and if so, who is the beneficiary. If I am named beneficiary, please send me the necessary forms and instructions for applying for benefits.

Sincerely yours,
Signature
Name typed/printed

Sample Claims Letter to Husband's Employer

Your name
Your street address
Your city, state, and zip code

Your telephone/fax numbers

Date

Employee Benefits Department
Corporation's name
Their street address
Their city, state, and zip code

re: Your husband's name

To Whom It May Concern:

This is to notify you that my husband, (husband's name), died on (date) in (city), (state).

His Social Security number was _____.

Please inform me regarding all employee benefits to which I am entitled as his beneficiary. Among them, any:

1. Unpaid salary
2. Unused vacation time
3. Health insurance under COBRA
4. Life insurance benefits
5. Pension and/or 401(k) benefits or other retirement plans
6. Stock options

Sincerely yours,
Signature
Name typed/printed

Chapter Five

MONEY FROM YOUR HUSBAND'S BUSINESS

The business of America is business.
—CALVIN COOLIDGE

Perhaps your husband was the type who participated in the American dream and owned his own business. Perhaps the two of you owned it together or with members of your family. Perhaps he was a partner in a small, closely held company. Whether it was a Mom-and-Pop deli or a large firm, there are a number of things you need to take into consideration.

Two items to check up on immediately are health insurance and pension benefits. First, find out if your health insurance premiums were paid by your husband's business and if coverage will continue. Second, if your husband was funding his own pension plan, find out who the plan administrator is and how you can file a claim as beneficiary. (The name of the plan administrator appears on the pension plan statements.)

Although it's impossible to anticipate every scenario you may face, here is some general advice. Add to it your own common sense.

If There Was a Buy-Sell Agreement

If your husband had a *buy-sell agreement*, the future of his interest in the business will be determined by the conditions stated in the agreement.

A buy-sell agreement is a legal document, drawn up by an attorney that provides for the succession of a business upon disability, retirement, or death of one of the owners. It spells out the terms under which a designated co-owner, loyal employee, spouse, heir, or other party will buy the deceased's interest in the business.

In other words, it guarantees a buyer for the deceased owner's interest. This means that the business can continue and that the deceased's beneficiaries will receive the fair market price for the deceased's interest.

Most buy-sell agreements include the actual purchase price or provide a formula for determining the price as well as the means for funding the purchase. Among the various funding options are _sinking funds_, loans, installment payments, and insurance on the owner's life.

Here's a typical example of a buy-sell agreement. Tom Jones, an accountant, and his partner drew up an agreement that would be implemented if one of three things occurred: death of either partner (funded by life insurance), disability of either partner or retirement (followed in two years by a lump-sum insurance payout), or departure of either partner (the remaining partner would pay for departing partner's share of the business according to a prearranged valuation formula).

If There Was No Buy-Sell Agreement

If your husband and his partners did not have a formal plan or life insurance, you might consider selling your husband's interest to the partners. However, you absolutely must not allow yourself to be pushed. I recommend that you wait several months before making a move one way or the other. During this time period, get the business appraised by an independent professional, but . . .

- Don't try to evaluate the business's worth yourself

- Don't ask friends for guesstimates

- Don't be bamboozled into accepting your husband's partner's evaluation

- Don't be rushed into making a decision

In the meantime, consult with both your accountant and lawyer. Ask them about turning to a business broker who may have an interested partner or a potential buyer.

If There Was Key-Man Insurance

Many partnerships have *key-man insurance*. This is life insurance on the "key" person in a business. In a small business, the key man could be the owner, founders, partners, or one or two key employees. The insurance is designed to cover those whose absence would ruin, or nearly ruin, the business.

The company, not an individual, purchases a life insurance policy, pays the premiums, and is the beneficiary of that policy. If the key person insured dies, the company then receives the insurance payout. This money is used to help the company survive by perhaps paying off debts, covering expenses, distributing money to investors, paying severance to employees, or, if need be, closing the business in an orderly manner. This type of policy also enables the surviving partner to hire someone to replace the deceased partner.

Coverage ranging from $100,000 to $250,000 typically costs $60 to $80 per month. However, coverage can be much higher; up to $1 million or more.

If You Inherit the Business Outright

According to the Boston-based Family Firm Institute, more than 90% of businesses in North America are family businesses; however, only 30% survive into the second generation, 12% into the third, and just 3% into a fourth generation.

SEVEN TIPS FOR WORKING WITH AN OUTSIDE ADVISER

1. Pick an experienced adviser. Ask what training he or she has had in the field and request names of clients as references.

2. Make certain the adviser is in no way affiliated with any family business members—either professionally or socially.

3. Select a person that all family business members trust. Take a vote.

4. Keep the relationship 100% professional. If you wish to have a breakfast or lunch meeting with outside counsel, include all family business members.

5. Draw up a written list of expectations and goals. Know what you want the outside counsel to accomplish. Among possible goals are drawing up a business plan, reducing debt, seeking funding, hiring new people, reducing staff, expanding, going public, or selling the business.

6. Encourage all family business members, including yourself, to keep an open mind and to listen carefully to what the adviser recommends.

7. Set a final decision date. Don't let the process drag on and on.

If you were working with your husband, you probably feel at ease assuming the responsibility of taking over the business. However, you may need to bring in someone else to take care of any areas of the business with which you're not familiar or if you're overwhelmed with work.

If you sense that there will be conflict in your family between those who work in the business and those who do not (or conflict for other reasons), I recommend that you hire a professional business adviser or counselor who is experienced in such affairs. Sometimes solutions are much more obvious to an outsider, especially during times of transition.

For More Help

The Family Firm Institute (617-482-3045 or www.ffi.org/looking/consult.cgi) has a list of small business consultants and counselors.

The Small Business Administration has a Women's Business Ownership division (202-205-6673 or www.sbaonline.sba.

gov/womeninbusiness) that counsels and advises women business owners.

The National Association of Female Executives (800-634-NAFE or www.nafe.com) is the largest association of female business owners.

Woman Owned Businesses (www.womanowned.com) links you to relevant articles and useful sources of information.

The American Society of Appraisers (800-272-8258 or www.appraisers. org) will give you a list of accredited appraisers in your area.

Family Business magazine (800-637-4464 or www.FamilyBusiness Magazine.com).

Entrepreneur magazine (800-274-6229 or www.entrepreneur.com).

The Survival Guide for Business Families: Critical Choices for Success, by Gerald Le Van (Routledge, 1998; www.levanco.com).

About Running a Small Business, Life Advice (800-MET-LIFE or www.lifeadvice.com).

Bottom Line

Once you've settled the details of your husband's business, you may decide you want to continue on, either with his business or one of your own. Don't think of it as a man's world. As Gloria Steinem said, "There are really not many jobs that actually require a penis or vagina, and all other occupations should be open to everyone."

Managing on Your Own

Chapter Six

TRACKING YOUR CASH FLOW

So far as my coin would stretch;
And where it would not,
I have used my credit.

—SHAKESPEARE

If you were the one who kept track of the cash in your family, you may not need to read this section. On the other hand, if your husband handled all or most of your money matters, it's now your turn to step up to the plate and learn how to do these things on your own. Believe me, it may not be as difficult as you imagine. You don't need a Ph.D. to set up a budget, balance a checkbook, and pay bills. But you do need to set aside some time—like a couple of Saturdays—to gather the facts.

Know Your Cash Flow

It all begins with knowing what your *cash flow* is. Think of yourself as a corporation. Corporations are required to track income and expenses and put these figures in their annual report. They're also required to be honest and not cook the books. When they do mess around with the facts—as in the case of Enron, WorldCom, and others—they get in trouble, and the public cries outrage.

So too, it is with your balance sheet. You might as well be as accurate as you can. You won't go to jail if you are not, and there's no one to cry outrage, but you also won't know the facts and could wind up in serious trouble, like bogged down with debt.

So, let's find out how much money you have coming in on a monthly basis. Then we'll take a look at your monthly expenses. Ideally your income will be greater than your expenses. If it is not, don't panic. We'll find ways to change that.

Begin by filling in the cash flow worksheet. I recommend that you use monthly dollar amounts since that is the way that most income and expenses are handled. For the purposes of filling out this form, divide by 12 any yearly income or expenses such as once-a-year bonus payment or annual taxes. You may not be certain about all the figures; you're allowed to estimate. No one is going to grade your paper. However, even the process of estimating expenses is a valuable one because it will make you more aware of what's taking place.

I can't emphasize enough that the key to taking charge of your financial life is to know the facts and then make a conscious decision to direct exactly where you want your money to go, rather than letting in gently sift away, unaccounted for.

Most of the required information will come from your tax return, canceled checks, bank statements, and your paycheck stubs. However, you may need to keep a daily expense diary for a month to learn where your so-called "walking around" money is going. Buy a small notebook, carry it at all times, and write down what you spend in cash every day. Then simply total it up at the end of the month. You may be quite surprised at the amount siphoned off into impulse purchases such as cappuccino-to-go, taxis, fast food, magazines, flowers, or snacks.

CASH FLOW WORKSHEET

PART I: INCOME (MONTHLY)

Salary . . . .$ _____

Bonus . . . .$ _____

Freelance, consulting, odd jobs . . . .$ _____

Social Security . . . .$ _____
(See Chapter 3 for more details.)

Pension benefits . . . .$ _____
(See Chapter 4 for more details.)

Annuity/Insurance . . . .$ _____
(See Chapter 4 for more details.)

Interest . . . .$ _____
(Savings, bonds)

Dividends . . . .$ _____
(Stocks)

Rental income . . . .$ _____

Other . . . .$ _____

Total Monthly Income $ _____

PART II: EXPENSES (MONTHLY)

Throughout, calculate expenses based on monthly expenditures even if you pay out on a daily, weekly, or annual basis. And don't forget to include any automatic savings or contributions for investing to which you've agreed. Although they are not really "expenses," they have an impact on your real cash flow.

Home Related
Mortgage/rent . . . .$ _____

Home equity loan . . . .$ _____

Property taxes . . . .$ _____

Condo or co-op fees . . . .$ _____

Insurance . . . .$ _____

Utilities . . . .$ _____
(phone, gas, electric, fuel, water, cable)

Repairs/Home improvement . . . .$ _____

Upkeep . . . .$ _____
(lawn, snow removal, pool, window washing, cleaning person)

Furniture . . . .$ _____

Total Monthly Home-Related Expenses $ _____

Day-to-Day Living
Food . . . .$ _____

Liquor . . . .$ _____

Dining out . . . .$ _____

Clothing . . . .$ _____

Cosmetics/Hair/Nails . . . .$ _____

Entertainment . . . .$ _____
         (movies, parties, vacation, tickets, tennis, golf, club dues)

Gym/Personal trainer/Health club . . . .$ _____

Gifts . . . .$ _____

Charitable contributions . . . .$ _____

Hobbies . . . .$ _____

Child care . . . .$ _____

Pets . . . .$ _____

Auto loan . . . .$ _____

Auto insurance . . . .$ _____

Auto oil, gas, repairs . . . .$ _____

Auto registration . . . .$ _____

Bus, taxi, train, shuttle . . . .$ _____

School tuition . . . .$ _____

Other educational expenses . . . .$ _____

Computer/Printer/Software . . . .$ _____

Credit card finance charges . . . .$ _____

Non-reimbursed medical bills . . . .$ _____

Non-reimbursed business expenses . . . .$ _____

Legal fees . . . .$ _____

Accounting fees . . . .$ _____

Total Monthly Day-to-Day Expenses $ _____

Loans, Payments, and Savings
Student loans . . . .$ _____

Credit card payments . . . .$ _____

Other . . . .$ _____

Total Monthly Loans and Payments $ _____

Medical and Insurance
Health insurance premiums . . . .$ _____

Dental insurance premiums . . . .$ _____

Life insurance premiums . . . .$ _____

Disability insurance premiums . . . .$ _____

Visits to doctors and dentists . . . .$ _____

Medicare payments . . . .$ _____

Eyeglasses/Contact lenses . . . .$ _____

Prescriptions . . . .$ _____

Other . . . .$ _____

Total Monthly Medical Expenses $ _____

Taxes
Federal income taxes . . . .$ _____

State income taxes . . . .$ _____

Local income taxes . . . .$ _____

Self-employed taxes . . . .$ _____

Total Monthly Taxes $ _____

Now you want to add up all your expenses:

Home Related . . . .$ _____

Day-to-Day Living . . . .$ _____

Loans, Payments, and Savings . . . .$ _____

Medical and Insurance . . . .$ _____

Taxes . . . .$ _____

                              Total Monthly Expenses $ _____

Next we subtract expenses from income:

                    Total Monthly Income . . . .$ _____

minus   *Total Monthly Expenses* . . . .$ _____

equals   *CASH FLOW* . . . .$ _____

Your Financial Balancing Act

Ideally, the bottom line here shows a surplus—that your income is greater than your expenses. Perhaps you're about breaking even. That's okay, too. If, on the other hand, your calculations show you're in debt, we need to find ways to spend less and/or to earn more.

There are some things we simply can't change, which are our *fixed expenses*. These remain constant factors in our life from month to month, such as mortgage payments, rent, life insurance premiums, child care, utilities, and property taxes.

One exception is, although you must keep up your insurance coverage, you certainly can shop around for a less expensive policy.

Where you can make a difference is with *variable expenses*: clothing, charitable donations, vacations, or snacks. Run down the list of variable expenses that follows. See where you can cut back—not necessarily cut out entirely, but reduce. I don't believe you should stop going to the health club or having your hair done, but you might want to go fewer times during the course of the month or switch to a less expensive place.

AN A TO Z OF VARIABLE EXPENSES

If your spending is outpacing your income, review this list and check off at least three items that can enable you to cut back. Instead of buying new books, for instance, head for your public library or thrift shop. If you love to read magazines, share subscriptions with a friend or colleague. If you're accustomed to shopping for clothes at expensive stores, switch to discount outlets and secondhand shops. If you enjoy having friends in for dinner, instead of providing the entire meal, turn it into a potluck affair. Before you buy a new red sweater, go through your drawers. Most of us have more than enough things in our closets and bureaus to last a lifetime. Chances are, you already own at least one red sweater.

☐ Books

☐ Cable TV

☐ Charitable donations

☐ Clothing

☐ Club dues and charges

☐ Collecting (antiques, art, collectibles)

☐ Cosmetics

☐ Drugstore purchases

☐ Dry cleaning

☐ Entertainment

☐ Flowers

☐ Gifts

☐ Groceries

☐ Hair salon

☐ Home improvements

☐ Housekeeper

☐ Landscaping and yard maintenance

☐ Liquor

☐ Magazine subscriptions

☐ Restaurant dining

☐ Transportation

☐ Vacations

Over the years, I've concluded that most women can reduce their spending without radically altering their lifestyle by making these four attitudinal changes. I'm sure you can add your own solutions to my list:

1. Make only preplanned shopping trips. Shop with a list and only for specific items in order to curtail impulse buying. And, never go grocery shopping when you're hungry.

2. Keep your emotions in rein. Spending habits are often driven by psychology. Refrain from buying when you're on an emotional high, when you're worried, or when you're angry. Don't go shopping with someone who spends more than you, tries to talk you into making purchases, or tells you every piece of clothing you try on looks great.

3. Don't try to keep up with the Joneses. There'll always be Joneses who have more income than you. Being competitive can lead to serious credit card debt.

4. Skip the malls. When you're feeling lonely, sad, or depressed, avoid department stores and boutiques. Instead go to a movie, listen to music, jog, take a walk, or call a friend.

ENJOYING BUDGET VICTORIES

Once you have set up a working budget (and only you can do this; no one can do it for you just as no one can lose weight for you), gradually treat yourself to a few extras. If you've saved according to plan or paid down a debt, for instance, reward yourself by dining with a friend or your children at a favorite restaurant or by going to a concert or baseball game. As you gain control over your cash flow, you can afford to be kinder and gentler to yourself, to enjoy your budgeting victories, and to have the sense of security that comes from being master of your financial universe.

THE THREE RULES OF SAFETY

As you move into your new life as a widow, keep these three safety rules in mind and review them every so often, especially as life's circumstances change:

1. Your monthly mortgage or rent should be less than 30% of your monthly net income.

2. Your total debt, including your mortgage, should not be more than 36% of your gross monthly income.

3. You should save 10% of your net income each month.

Buttoning Down: 12 Ways to Save More Than Pennies

Small things do add up. Making some of these minor but easy changes in how you live will put more money in your savings account:

1. Don't smoke. Besides jeopardizing your health, smoking is very expensive, especially if you live in New York or New Jersey where a pack of cigarettes now costs as much as $7.50. If you smoke two packs a day, that's a whopping $15. Over the course of a week, lighting up can cost you $105. Plus, nonsmokers get lower rates on health and automobile insurance.

2. Dine at home more. Restaurants are one of the biggest nonessential items in the American budget. If you don't have time to cook or you're the type that burns the toast, pick up food at your local Chinese or other inexpensive restaurant on the way home from work. You'll save at least 15% because you won't have to tip the waiter or pay for soft drinks, wine, or beer. And you'll probably have leftovers for another meal. Of course it's a given you'll dine out at least once a week and when you do, think about skipping the starter and dessert and, if you drink, sticking

with the house wine. The markup on alcohol is way over 100%, even at a Mom-and-Pop place. Then come back home for coffee and dessert and count up the savings.

3. Pump your own gas. Depending on where you live, you can save 10 cents a gallon just by getting out of the car and using the self-service pump.

4. Drive at the speed limit and save on gas. Traveling at 65 mph versus 55 mph increases fuel consumption by 20%. And, by not speeding, you're less likely to get pulled over and ticketed.

5. Clip coupons. If you use just $25 worth of food and over-the-counter drug coupons a month, you can save $300 a year.

6. Brown bag it. If you spend $8 a day on a sandwich, coffee or soda, and a candy bar—and that's being modest—that adds up to $2,000 year, assuming two weeks off for vacation. That's not counting those costly mid-morning cappuccinos-to-go and the late-afternoon quick-energy chips, pretzels, and ice cream. Try bringing lunch from home three or more days a week and put the money you save into a savings account.

7. Car pool or take public transportation. Ford, GM, and Toyota love the fact that everyone in this country over age 16 feels entitled to drive their SUV or 4 x 4 door to door—whether it's to school, the mall, a baseball game, or work. You can help the environment and your wallet by commuting with several other people. Or, compare the cost of running a car (gas, repairs, parking fees, upkeep, insurance, payments) with taking the train, subway, or bus. Keep in mind that the two cheapest means of getting from point A to point B—walking and biking—are also the healthiest.

If you think giving up your door-to-door lifestyle is out of the question, test the water by trying a less expensive alternative once a week for a month and see how it goes. You may find it's much less stressful to read, play cards, or snooze on the train or bus than it is to be stuck in gridlock.

If you're an urbanite, track the number of taxi rides you take during a one-week period. Compare the total cost with how much the bus or subway fare would be for the same number of trips. The average cab ride in most cities is $5 to $8. The average subway or bus is $1.50 to $2.00. Need I say more?

8. Talk less. Make sure you have the cheapest telephone calling plan. And if you make a lot of long-distance calls, consider getting a prepaid phone card.

9. Stash the plastic. If you leave your ATM, credit, and debit cards; checkbook; and most of your cash at home when you go out, it will be difficult for you to make those costly impulse purchases. Instead, carry just the amount of cash you expect to use for the day, plus one bank check or a traveler's check and one credit card for emergencies.

10. Avoid bank fees. Charges for check processing and ATM transactions add up. Shop around for a bank that offers one or both for free.

11. Toss the catalogs. When they arrive in your mailbox, don't even peek inside; doing so opens the door of temptation. And get off catalog mailing lists by writing to:

Direct Mail Association
Telephone Preference Service
P.O. Box 1559
Carmel, NY 10512
www.dmaconsumers.org/offmailinglist.html (this website charges a fee)

12. Run an energy check. Call your utility company and ask if it has time-of-day pricing. With this type of plan, you will be granted lower rates if you do not use your appliances during peak periods—for example, if you run the dishwasher and do the laundry after 8 P.M. during the week, when power usage is at its lowest. Most consumers using the time-of-day pricing system save between 10% and 30%.

And, ask your utility company to give you a free energy

checkup. Most will come to your house, do a thorough inspection, and then recommend specific ways to reduce your bill. Checkups typically result in 7% to 25% lower monthly bills.

For More Help

Energy Savers, available from the U.S. Department of Energy (www. eren.doe.gov/energy_savers.com), is full of useful tips.

Bottom Line

As you work on paying bills and living within a budget, you may want to put your credit cards in the freezer and keep in mind the words that appear on a sign in an Arkansas diner: "In God we trust—all others pay cash."

Chapter Seven

SETTING UP A NEW SYSTEM: BILLS AND CREDIT CARDS

Money is a terrible master but an excellent servant.
—P. T. Barnum

Now that you've got a fairly good idea about the amount of money coming in and going out each month, let's go on to talk about how to handle other financial issues so that you master money and not vice versa.

Paying Your Bills

Getting started is simple. Go through all piles of paper or filing folders and extract all outstanding bills. Put them on your desk or table and then divide them into three different groups:

1. Your personal bills

2. Bills in both your names

3. Your husband's bills

You are legally responsible for paying your own personal bills and any bills or debts jointly held. The estate should pay those bills belonging solely to your husband, using the checking account you opened for that purpose.

$TIP: As you review bills sent to your husband, scrutinize them very carefully. If any are from an unknown source, do not pay them. Call and ask for a written itemization of the bill. Pass this information on to your attorney. This is one of those times when unscrupulous people come out of the woodwork and take advantage of widows, often billing them for things their husband never purchased or ordered.

Make a list of all bills in each of the three categories, noting who is owed money, the amount owed, the minimum payment required, and the due date. If you have sufficient income, then paying the bills will only be time consuming, not burdensome and you can skip to the next section. On the other hand, if you don't have enough money, you'll need to set priorities in paying your debts.

However, you must make every effort to make your monthly payments on time. If you don't, you'll not only be hit with hefty interest charges and late fees but your credit record will be severely tarnished, something that could haunt you for many years to come.

BILLS THAT MUST BE PAID

Your mortgage (or rent) must be your number one check. Second, pay your utilities—gas, electric, water, telephone—followed by your health and homeowners insurance premiums. Next in importance, are your car payment and any other car-related expenses.

THREE STEPS TO HANDLING CREDIT CARD BILLS

Step 1. If you have one credit card bill with just a small amount due, pay it off in total. You'll find it psychologically very rewarding, rather like losing the first two or three pounds when you go on a diet. Then, take that card out of your wallet. Put it in the freezer or cut it up.

Step 2. Your next goal is to pay down the card with the highest interest rate. When you've wiped out that debt, move on to the next highest-rate card. The reason behind this advice: when you're not paying your bill in full every month, much of your check may be going toward finance charges rather than paying for the items and services you purchased. Unless you pay off your debt, you'll merely be treading water.

Step 3. Finally, if you cannot pay off the entire amount due, make certain that you at least make the minimum payment to avoid damaging your *credit report*.

I urge you to work very hard at eliminating credit card debt. The interest rates on unpaid balances are simply outrageous and they're not tax deductible as is the interest on a mortgage payment. You know the rest.

If You Can't Pay Your Bills

It happens. In fact, it's not at all unusual for widows, who no longer have their husband's salary, to find themselves short of cash. Don't feel you are the only one in this situation. You're definitely not.

Group together those bills for which you don't have money to pay. Figure out how much you owe and how long it will take you to get back on schedule. Then call each creditor. Gerri Detweiler, the nation's guru on consumer credit and author of *The Ultimate Credit Handbook,* says that nine out of ten creditors will negotiate new repayment schedules with those who are having trouble paying their bills.

Place these calls right away. You want to be the one who makes the first move. Don't wait until you start receiving dunning calls or letters from bill collectors. Ask for a bereavement *grace period*. Explain what has happened, that you realize you owe this certain amount of money, and that you plan to pay it over time. Indicate that you will be sending so much a month until you have made a financial recovery.

If you have any problems with the first person you talk with, you get stonewalled, or you are told there's nothing that can be done, ask to speak with the supervisor. It is indeed possible to negotiate lower payments stretched out over a long time period. And don't be pressured into paying more than you can really afford.

Make a note of the first and last name of the person you speak with, the date of the call, and the terms of agreement. Then send a typed letter confirming the new agreement to that person. Keep a copy for your files. (I am advising you to ask for the person's last name because so often at the other end of a toll-free call we find we are talking with John or Jane and in large companies, it's impossible to track down someone by first name only.)

CHANGING CREDIT CARD NAMES

If a credit card account is in your husband's name only, you are not liable for his charges. Creditors, however, can file claims against your husband's estate for payment, if payment has not been made (see Chapter 2) If you live in a _community property state_, however, the regulations vary widely, so check with your attorney.

If your credit cards were in your husband's name because he had the earning power and you had permission to use them, I recommend that you wait until you have opened at least one credit card account in your own name before notifying issuers of your husband's cards of his death.

On the other hand, if you were a cosigner on joint accounts with your husband and you have enough income to handle any bills you undertake, then notify the creditors that the accounts should be changed to reflect only your name. That will give you credit in your own name, which brings us to the next important point.

GETTING CREDIT IN YOUR NAME

As a woman on your own, you should make it a priority to apply for credit in your own name. Don't continue on forever using the same credit cards as you did before your husband died. If you do, the good credit rating will continue to be in your deceased husband's name and not yours.

Should you wish to buy a house or other piece of real estate, take out a home equity loan, or get a business or auto loan, you'll need credit in your own name.

And the reality of life is that credit cards come in handy, especially in an emergency—if the car breaks down—as well as when you need to buy an airline or train ticket, book a hotel room, or purchase other large-ticket items. In fact, it is unrealistic to think of life today without a credit card.

Different cards charge different interest rates, so try to get as low a rate as possible. In addition to reading the offers that come in the mail, log on to www.bankrate.com. Here you'll find a nationwide list of credit cards with low interest rates and annual fees. As of late fall 2002, Wachovia Bank was issuing a Visa card with a 4.75% rate and an annual fee of $98 while Pulaski Bank & Trust had a Visa with only a $35 annual fee but the interest rate was higher, 5.50%. You'll also find a great deal of helpful information on this site, including articles on how to get a card if you've never had one and how to clean up your credit report.

NOTIFY THE MAJOR CREDIT AGENCIES

Once you have established credit in your own name, I recommend that you notify the three major *credit bureaus* (listed on page 70) that your husband has died. This puts an end to his receiving offers for pre-approved credit cards and pre-authorized checks for loans. You don't want someone else to have access to this information and open accounts in his name. It would not be your legal responsibility to handle such charges, but it would be emotionally painful and difficult to deal with.

Credit bureaus, which are also referred to as credit reporting agencies, are for-profit companies that collect, package, and sell information about our financial lives to lenders, employers, insurance agencies, and others. These paying customers use the information to determine if they will offer loans and other services to specific people.

A good credit report is often a determining factor in whether or not you can get a mortgage or other type of loan or credit cards with favorable rates and terms.

The three major agencies to inform are:

- Experian: 888-397-3742 or www.experian.com

- TransUnion: 800-916-8800 or www.transunion.com

- Equifax: 800-685-1111 or www.equifax.com

> **$TIP:** If you have Internet access, TrueCredit (www.truecredit.com) offers for a small fee all three national credit bureau reports in one, easy-to-read document.

IF YOU CANNOT GET CREDIT

If you are unable to get a credit card on your own, you have several possibilities. Your local department store may give you a card, especially if you've been a loyal customer—a fact that you'll point out to them. A bank (perhaps your own) may give you a _secured card_. This type of card is linked to your savings account and if you fail to make your payments, the company issuing the card may claim the money in your account. This arrangement provides some degree of protection to the card issuer and allows them to take on riskier credit card applicants.

Another possibility is a _debit card_, a bank-issued Visa or Master-Card. It too offers the convenience of a credit card but eliminates your ability to overspend and run up debt because purchases are deducted electronically from your checking account. (Your bank ATM card is also a type of debit card, but not accepted by most merchants for purchases.)

After you've established credit in your own name, you can apply for a traditional credit card with more favorable terms.

Another way to live within your means when it comes to plastic is with a _charge card_, such as American Express. With this type of card, you are legally required to pay your balance in full each month. And, there is no line of credit, which you can continually tap.

For More Help

Bank Rate Monitor (www.bankrate.com) is the number one source for finding credit, debit, and secured cards.

For an explanation of credit cards, late fees, and grace periods, log on to the "Stay Savvy about Your Credit" section at Quicken's site, www.quicken.com/banking_and_credit/credit_cards.

About Having Credit Problems, Life Advice (800-MET-LIFE or www. lifeadvice.com).

The Ultimate Credit Handbook, by Gerri Detweiler (Penguin Books), covers everything you need to know about handling credit cards, loans, and various types of debts. Detweiler's website (www.ultimatecredit. com) also addresses many of the questions women have about credit.

Read Chapter 5, "Solving Debt & Credit Problems," in *Personal Finance for Dummies,* by Eric Tyson (IDG Books Worldwide, 2000).

Bottom Line

Now that you've set up an easy-to-follow system for paying bills on time, you will no longer be overwhelmed by debt, which Thomas Carlyle defined as " a bottomless sea."

Chapter Eight

YOUR HEALTH INSURANCE

To wish to be healthy is a part of being healthy.
— SENECA

One of the risks we cannot afford to take in life is being without health insurance. To do so is to court both financial and medical disaster. We all know that, yet many people decide to forgo insurance because it is so expensive. So let's look at both the various ways you may be entitled to coverage.

All About COBRA

If your husband worked for a company that had 20 or more employees, I have excellent news. This size company must provide health care for its employees. And, under the terms of the federal Consolidated Omnibus Reconciliation Act, popularly known as COBRA, widows and their dependent children must be offered coverage for 36 months after their husband's death.

The downside is that you have to pay the monthly premiums. And, although they are almost always considerably lower than if you purchase your own policy, they will not be cheap. If you're young and healthy, plan on paying $200 to $300 per month. You'll pay more if you're older and/or have a *preexisting condition*.

COBRA in fact is especially valuable if you do have a preexisting condition; you not only continue the coverage you had under your husband's plan, but you cannot be dropped. Nor can the insurance company single you out for a rate increase should your care become increasingly expensive.

You have 60 days in which to decide whether or not to stay with your husband's plan. It's important to pay attention to that 60-day window of opportunity because once it is closed, you cannot get coverage under COBRA. Be sure you ask your husband's employer about COBRA if you have not heard from the company. Even if you don't have the first month's premium in hand, fill out the COBRA form anyway and mail or fax it in. You will then be given another 45 days in which to pay the first premium. (The form is available from your husband's employer.)

Caution: If you miss the premium payment date by one day, you officially lose coverage, although you might be able to plead forgiveness. But don't count on it.

Purchasing Individual Coverage

If you are working and already have coverage or if you can sign up for coverage, compare the cost and extent of coverage offered by your employer with what you would receive via COBRA. If your coverage is superior and if your job is stable (a critical factor), then stick with your plan. Remember, COBRA, even if it is cheaper, eventually runs out.

If your husband worked for a small company, and therefore COBRA is not an option, or you're an independent contractor, consultant, or freelancer, you'll need to purchase your own coverage. However, before signing up:

1. Contact any professional associations or labor unions in your field. A great many provide group type insurance policies for active members. So do social clubs, sororities, religious groups, local trade associations, and other organizations. For example, the American Society of Journalists & Authors (212-997-0947 or

www.asja.org) offers coverage to members as does the Church Pension Group (800-223-6602 or www.cpg.org) and Chorus America (202-331-7577 or http://chorusamerica.org/health_ins. shtml). The National Association for the Self-Employed (800-232-NASE or www.nase.org) provides group-rate health insurance for freelancers, consultants, and other self-employed people. This 20-year-old organization also provides online tax advice from volunteer CPAs.

2. Check out policies at www.eHealthInsurance.com. This is not an insurance company but rather a go-between, a sort of Internet-based insurance broker. It has links to more than a hundred insurance companies in all 50 states. You can quickly compare the benefits and costs of five different plans and even apply online if you wish. The firm also has experts you can consult with by phone. Be sure to read the "Frequently Asked Questions" before signing up for any policy. (If you do not have Internet access, an independent insurance agent can provide quotes.)

3. Look into state-sponsored plans. If you are denied coverage, you might be eligible for a state plan, often referred to as a *high-risk insurance pool*. You can also turn to a state pool if after the 36 months of COBRA coverage you do not have a new source of coverage. However, premiums are high and waiting lists are long. Details and phone numbers of individual state programs can be found at www.insure.com/health/highriskpool.html. (If you do not have Internet access, you can check with your state insurance regulator. A complete list is available in the *Consumer Action Handbook*, mentioned in the introduction to this book or in the government pages of the phone book.)

4. Finally, if you have car, liability, disability, or household coverage with a company that also offers health insurance, contact your agent or the company directly. You may qualify for coverage along with a small break on premiums.

Your comprehensive health policy should:

- Cover at least 80% of both your medical and hospital bills once you meet the *deductible*.

- Have a cap on your annual out-of-pocket *copayments* that's between $1,000 and $2,000.

- Be renewable. You don't want the policy canceled if you suddenly become very ill.

- Give reduced premiums to nonsmokers.

- Not exclude or limit coverage for preexisting conditions.

Disability Insurance

If you are working, you should also have disability insurance. (In fact, you must be working in order to qualify.) It is as important as your health coverage; a recent study by the Health Insurance Association of America indicates that 30% of Americans between the ages of 35 and 65 will be disabled for 90 days during their lifetime.

Disability insurance provides income when you are unable to work due to sickness, an accident, or injury. Should one of these events occur, your income would be reduced, perhaps substantially, but your cost of living would remain the same or even go up. And, you no longer have a second income to fall back on. Although most employers provide benefits, they are often not enough to cover all your expenses if you're unable to work.

SEVEN THINGS TO LOOK FOR IN A DISABILITY POLICY

1. Renewable. The policy should be one without a cancellation clause and should be guaranteed renewable.

2. Benefits. It should replace 60% to 80% of your net income.

3. Own occupation coverage. It should pay out when you cannot work *at your own occupation,* rather than pay out when you cannot do *any* type of work.

4. Cost of living. It should have a rider to protect the benefits from inflation.

5. Option to increase. You want a future insurability option to boost insurance as your income increases, regardless of the status of your health.

6. Partial payouts. Insist on getting partial payouts for partial disabilities.

7. Premium waiver. You want a policy that eliminates premium payments while you are disabled.

For More Help

COBRA Health Plan Advice for Individuals & Small Businesses (www.cobrahealth.com) will answer most of your questions.

The Health Insurance Resource Center (www.healthinsurance.org), a nonprofit group, has excellent consumer tips and specific advice on what to do if you're turned down because of a medical condition. It also provides quotes for self-employed people and links to the 30 states that have high-risk pools.

Quotesmith (800-556-9393 or www.quotesmith.com) will search its database for the names of several health and disability insurers that meet your conditions. The service is free.

Insure (www.insure.com/disability/longtermdisability.html) has useful information on disability insurance.

Medicare

Many women (and men too) think that Medicare will take care of everything and everyone in their older years. Not true. Medicare does not provide total coverage, a fact that often comes as a great shock. Let's take a look at what it does and does not cover and if you are eligible.

Medicare is a government-run health care program that guarantees older people affordable health care. It is administered by the U.S. Department of Health & Human Services and provides primary health insurance for most people 65 and older as well as for the chronically disabled.

WHO IS ELIGIBLE?

You can get Medicare if:

- You are at least 65 years old.
- You (or your husband) have paid into Social Security for at least 40 quarters or ten years.
- You paid into the program but have been disabled for a minimum of two years; in other words, a disabled person under 65 may be eligible.
- You are a kidney dialysis or kidney transplant patient.

Some women who are 65 or older but do not meet these eligibility requirements may purchase Medicare by applying to the Social Security Administration (800-325-0778). You have to be a U.S. citizen or permanent resident. The cost ranges from $174 to $316 per month depending upon the length of coverage.

The government does not tell you about your right to coverage nor will it notify you that it's time to apply. You must take the initiative and put in your application about three months before the month you turn 65. Don't drop your other health insurance until your Medicare benefits kick in, which is on the first day of your birthday month—that is, if your birthday is May 22, benefits begin on May 1. If you are already on Social Security, there is no application process; it is automatic. Details are available at: 800-MEDICARE or www.medicare.gov/basics/socialsecurity.com.

WHAT MEDICARE COVERS

Medicare comes in two parts: hospital insurance and medical insurance.

Hospital insurance pays a portion of inpatient hospital care, some home health care, and inpatient care in a skilled nursing facility after a hospital stay or a hospice stay.

It pays for all medically necessary inpatient hospital care for the first 60 days minus a deductible ($840 in 2003) for each benefit period. Coverage includes a semiprivate room, all meals, special and intensive care units, coronary care units, regular nursing services, and drugs while in the hospital.

Hospital insurance will also pay for up to a hundred days in a skilled nursing facility. The first 20 days are fully covered, but for days 21 through a hundred, a daily copayment of $101.50 is required. The patient must have been hospitalized first for at least three days and then admitted to the nursing facility within 30 days after leaving the hospital in order to qualify.

Home health care services can last as long as you are under a physician's plan of care and basically confined to your home. Physical, occupational, and speech therapy as well as the services of a home health aide are available. And, fortunately, a previous hospital stay is not required.

The Medicare hospice program includes both home care and inpatient care. The patient must be certified by a physician as being terminally ill with a life expectancy of six months or less.

Note: You are automatically enrolled in the hospital insurance program when you reach 65 if you are receiving Social Security benefits. And, as long as you are, you do not have to pay for hospital insurance coverage.

Medical insurance, on the other hand, is an optional or voluntary program. If you pay a monthly premium, you are entitled to reimbursement for certain things, including outpatient hospital services and other medical services, medical supplies, durable equipment, therapy, and ambulance transportation when other types of transportation are health threatening. The annual deductible is $100. Once you have met the deductible, medical insurance pays 80% of the Medicare-approved amount and you then pay the other 20%.

Most people who enroll in the medical insurance program have their monthly premiums deducted from their Social Security, Railroad Retirement, or civil service checks. Those who do not receive these payments are billed on a quarterly basis. As of 2003, the monthly premium is $58.70.

You should apply for medical insurance coverage three months before turning 65. That is when the initial enrollment period starts; it continues for seven months. Don't put off enrollment; medical insurance premiums go up 10% a year for each year you delay enrollment. (Exception: if after 65 you're still working or have group health coverage.)

WHAT MEDICARE DOES NOT COVER

Medicare does not cover the following:

- Long-term nursing home or custodial care, such as assisted living

- Routine physicals

- Dental services and dentures

- Prescription drugs, except for hospital patients

- Eye exams and glasses

- Hearing tests and hearing aids

- Cost of a physician above Medicare's approved dollar amount

- Care outside the United States

- A physician's care on a cruise ship once it is beyond the U.S. territorial waters

- Private duty nursing

- Private hospital rooms (generally not covered)

MEDICARE+ CHOICE PLANS

Many areas throughout the country are now offering a newer type Medicare option. Called Medicare+ Choice, it includes Medicare

Managed Care Plans, which are very similar to HMOs, and Medicare fee-for-service plans offered by private insurance companies. Each of these plans continue to provide Medicare hospital and medical coverage plus some extra benefits.

If you have Medicare+, you do not need to buy the Medigap plan explained below.

Medigap Insurance

Now that you have a general idea of what Medicare does and does not pay for, you need to take a look at _Medigap insurance_, also known as Medicare Supplemental Insurance. It is provided by private insurance companies and designed to cover what Medicare does not. It picks up most out-of-pocket costs—but not all. It does not cover eye care, dental care, hearing aids, private nurses, or long-term health care.

You are not required to sign up for Medigap insurance but, with the continually rising cost of medical expenses, it may be a good idea.

You are guaranteed access to Medigap coverage if you act within six months of enrolling in Medicare medical insurance. This period is known as _open enrollment_ and, during that time, you can purchase Medigap insurance from any insurance company selling coverage in your state. After signing up, you have 30 days to review the policy. If you are not pleased with it, you can get a full refund.

Be sure to sign up right away; it pays to do so. During the enrollment period, you cannot be denied coverage because of any current or past health problems as long as you have had continuous health insurance coverage for the previous six months. During the open enrollment period, a Medigap provider cannot charge you more based on your health situation.

There are ten standardized plans, labeled A through J, with A being the most basic coverage and J the most comprehensive. Every insurer must sell A coverage, which picks up most out-of-pocket co-payments of hospital charges and doctor bills.

Most Medigap policies are guaranteed renewable. That's very important. You don't want the insurance company to refuse to renew your policy as you get older and perhaps frailer. However, companies can refuse to renew if you don't pay the premiums or if you lied on your application. So, pay on time and tell the truth.

COMPARISON SHOP

Because Medigap plans A through J are standardized, the benefits under each type of plan are the same, no matter which insurance company you use. However, service may differ as well as charges. So, do take time to comparison shop. Start with AARP if you are a member.

> **$TIP: For a list of providers in your state, go to www.medicare.gov. On the home page, you'll find a "Medicare Personal Plan Finder."**

I recommend that you call three companies and ask for quotes. If you are a nonsmoker, find out if you will be given a discount. You also want to know if the cost is the same for everyone or if costs are age-based and go up automatically as you get older.

Since 1982, Medicare recipients have had another option: Medicare Health Maintenance Organizations (HMOs). The government pays an HMO a certain amount of money annually for each Medicare recipient who signs up. In exchange, the HMO offers participants the full range of Medicare-covered services and in some cases, additional benefits.

A WORD ABOUT FRAUD

The persons least able to handle the Medicare paperwork—the elderly or the very ill—are often responsible for doing so. This has contributed to opportunities for fraud and just plain, nonfraudulent old-fashioned mistakes. Among the things to watch out for:

- Doctors who charge Medicare patients for office visits and then bill Medicare for the same service

- Medical equipment suppliers who provide more expensive equipment than is really needed

- Those that provide lower cost or used equipment and yet bill for higher cost or new equipment

You can report suspected fraud and get assistance from the U.S. Department of Health & Human Resources tip line at 800-447-8477 or by email at htips@os.dhhs.gov.

For More Help

Social Security has a number of brochures on Medicare plus a publication called *The Medicare Handbook*. For free copies, stop in at your local Social Security office, call 800-772-1213, or log on to www.ssa.gov.

The Medicare Program (800-MEDICARE or www.medicare.gov) has detailed information as well as the number for your state health insurance program.

The Guide To Health Insurance for People with Medicare is available for free from the U.S. Department of Health & Human Services, 877-696-6775.

The Center for Medicare & Medicaid Services (800-267-2323 or http://cms.hhs.gov/medicaid/default.asp) is the best source on Medicare.

Seniors Source (www.seniors.gov) provides information on health and insurance as well as other topics, including key legislation.

COVERAGE FOR LOW-INCOME WIDOWS

Single people with low incomes (the amount changes periodically) can apply for assistance from one of two federal programs: the Specified Low-Income Medicare Beneficiary (SLIMB) or Qualifying Individuals (QI). These programs are both administered locally and they pay your monthly Medicare Part B premium.

For information, call the U.S. Administration on Aging (800-677-1116) and ask for a local office. Or, check Medicare's website (www.medicare.gov).

Medicaid

Medicaid is the health assistance program designed specifically for the poor. Although federal money is involved, it is administered by each state and therefore benefits vary widely.

Although it is a program for low-income Americans, many middle-income people manage to qualify—some by actually spending all of their money on nursing home bills, which is known as becoming medically needy, and others by using sophisticated strategies to transfer their assets, either to other family members or into irrevocable trusts.

WHAT MEDICAID COVERS

The Medicaid health care programs cover a broad range of services. Federal law mandates certain benefits. That is, if the state wants federal matching funds, it must offer the following to "needy populations":

- Inpatient and outpatient hospital services

- Services of a doctor

- Prenatal care

- Vaccines for children

- Physician services

- Nursing facilities for people 21 or older

- Family planning services and supplies

- Rural health clinic services

- Pediatric and family nurse practitioner services

- Nurse-midwife services

- Some ambulatory services

- Early and periodic screening, diagnostic, and treatment services for children under age 21

Depending upon the state where you live, other services may be provided.

WHO IS ELIGIBLE?

Eligibility, like benefits, varies from state to state. If, for example, you live in New York State and you are the only person in your family, you may have up to $635 in monthly income and $3,800 in resources and still qualify. For a two-person family, the figures rise to $925 per month and $5,550 in resources. You may also own a car, your house, and personal property. The eligibility rules are easier for pregnant women, children, and the disabled.

To qualify, you will need to verify your age and show proof of residency, citizenship, marital status, income, and other resources. You will be asked to disclose all financial records, such as bank statements; savings accounts; a list of stocks, bonds, and mutual funds; a real estate inventory; plus an explanation of all transactions or transfers over a certain dollar amount.

YOUR HOME

All states exempt a primary residence as an asset as long as you are living in the home. If you leave your home for a nursing home, the state may or may not continue to exempt it.

TRANSFERRING ASSETS

If you are considering transferring assets to another family member in order to qualify, consult an attorney who specializes in elder law. The National Academy of Elder Law Attorneys in Tucson will provide the names of several in your area. Call: 520-881-4005 or log on to www.naecla.com.

Two critical things you want to discuss with an expert are any penalties for transferring assets to someone other than a spouse and how long the lookback period is—that is, the time you must wait after giving assets away before becoming eligible for Medicaid.

THE MEDICAID INCOME-ONLY TRUST

Another topic to discuss with an elder care lawyer is the Medicaid Income-Only Trust, an estate-planning tool. It is funded with the assets of the grantor, which in this case would be you. The grantor retains for life the stream of income from dividends and interest but has no right to any of the principal.

The trust can hold stocks, bonds, savings accounts, your house, co-op, or condominium. If it includes your house, make certain the trust has a provision so you have the right to live in the house for the rest of your life.

For More Help

The Center for Medicare & Medicaid Services (CMS) (877-267-2323 or www.cms.hhs.gov) offers a brochure *Medicaid: A Brief Summary.*

Health Insurance Information (www.healthinsuranceinfo.net/index. htm) lists the qualification requirements for all 50 states.

Long-Term Care Insurance

According to those experts who love to crunch numbers, it is likely that 20% of Americans age 65 or older will live in a nursing home. Today, the average cost of these homes ranges from $35,295 to $98,185 a year. Living a long time could turn out to be a very expensive proposition!

Do not make the common mistake of assuming that Medicare will pay for this. As you now know, it will not. Medicare only covers short-term stays (up to 90 days in a skilled nursing home) and then only if you go into a facility immediately after leaving the hospital. It then pays a small percentage for a limited number of days. Nor will supplemental Medicare policies (the Medigap policies discussed earlier in this chapter) pick up coverage.

That leaves Medicaid and private insurance. Long-term policies provide either a fixed dollar amount per day, called an indemnity pol-icy, or they reimburse the policyholder for expenses, up to a certain set amount, known as a reimbursement policy.

Coverage, which is not cheap, depends on these factors: your age when you apply, your health, the benefits you want, how long the benefits will be covered, and the time you wait until payments begin. To qualify, you must be in relatively good health and the younger you are when you buy coverage, the lower the premiums.

If, for example, you are 75 and in good health, premiums will run somewhere in the neighborhood of $177 to $605 per month for a full coverage life-long policy. The same coverage for a 50 year old, also in good health, is only $45 to $163 per month.

> $TIP: Before buying a policy, find out the cost of nursing home care in the area where you live. Make certain the size of the benefit meets local costs. Benefits can range anywhere from $100 a day to $150 per day.

TEN THINGS TO LOOK FOR IN A POLICY

The National Association of Insurance Commissioners recommends that the policy include:

1. Alzheimer's. Coverage for Alzheimer's or a similar disease af-ter the policy is purchased.

2. Everyday functions and/or assisted living. The policy should cover you should you not be able to bathe, dress, or eat on your own as well as move in and out of a wheelchair and bed. Assisted living coverage is key; these facilities provide a transitional place between home and a nursing home.

3. Home health care coverage. You also want coverage regard-less of whether you are hospitalized first or go directly into a nursing home. The policy should pay for licensed agencies to pro-

vide the home care, with you or your children being the ones to select the home care people.

4. Payout time. Also referred to as the "elimination period," this is the length of time you have been in a nursing home or receiving home care before the insurance company starts paying benefits. It's usually between 20 and 100 days. The shorter the period, the higher the annual premium. Select the shortest period you can afford.

5. Length of benefits. This involves a bit of a gamble. The average stay in a nursing home is approximately three years, but many women, in particular, are living in nursing homes longer than that. Obviously, coverage for five years will cost more than for three.

6. Inflation adjustment. Nursing home costs continually rise. You want some safeguard against inflation. Most riders provide coverage for 5% to 7% inflation per year.

7. Waiver of premium. Make certain the premiums are waived once you begin using the policy.

8. A better policy. If the insurance company later on markets a better policy, you want the option for retroactive coverage.

9. "Front-end" underwriting. This means the insurance company reviews your health *before* it issues the policy. With back-end underwriting, the policy determines if it will pay after you file a claim. Avoid the back-end version at all costs.

10. A free look. You want the right to cancel a policy within 30 days for a premium refund if you decide the policy is not appropriate.

> $TIP: Buy a policy only from a financially sound company that is rated A or A+ by A. M. Best and AA from Standard & Poor's. These ratings are available from each insurance company or agent. You can also get ratings from:

- A. M. Best: 908-439-2200 or www.ambest.com

- Standard & Poor's Insurance Rating Service: 212-438-2400 or email ratings_request@standardandpoors.com

Protection If You Forget to Pay Your Premiums

The National Association of Insurance Commissioners (NAIC) recommends that all insurers allow policy buyers to designate up to three people to be notified if a policy is about to lapse because of nonpayment. The designees are not liable for payment. For details on your state's rulings, log on to www.naic.com.

For More Help

A Shopper's Guide to Long-Term Care Insurance, from National Association of Insurance Commissioners (816-842-3600 or www.naic. org). On the website, click on "Publications Catalog" and then "Consumer Information." The book is $6 if you order it by phone but free if you download it from the site.

United Seniors Health Cooperative (800-637-2604) has an updated edition of the popular book *Long-Term Care Planning: A Dollar and Sense Guide.* It is $19.50 including shipping. Ask for Item #LTC. This group is a nonprofit, membership-based organization that has been publishing unbiased consumer information since 1986. It was founded by Dr. Arthur Flemming, former Secretary of the U.S. Department of Health, Education, and Welfare; and Esther Peterson, former White House Affairs Adviser.

Choosing a Quality Nursing Home is available for free from The American Association of Homes and Services for the Aging (www. aahsa.org).

A Consumer's Guide to Long-Term Care Insurance is free from the Health Insurance Association of America (202-783-2242 or www. hiaa.org).

About Long-Term Care, Life Advice (800-MET-LIFE or www.metlife. com).

Bottom Line

In addition to having health insurance, you can also protect yourself by living a healthy life—watching your weight, getting exercise, and not smoking or doing drugs. Mark Twain put it well when asked what he thought contributed to good health: "To eat what you don't want, drink what you don't like and do what you'd rather not."

Chapter Nine

YOUR LIFE, CAR, AND HOME INSURANCE

Life consists not in holding good cards but in playing those you do hold well.

—AMBROSE BIERCE

In the previous chapter, we updated your health, disability, and long-term care insurance. But there are several other types of coverage you may need, such as life, homeowners, and car insurance. If you do not have dependents or do not own a car, you can skip the first two. But if you are a renter, you must read the homeowners section; your landlord, no matter how kindly a person, does not carry insurance on your antiques, appliances, artwork, clothes, computer, furniture, or jewelry.

Life Insurance

Despite what an insurance agent may tell you, not every widow in the world really needs life insurance. If you do not have dependents, you're independently wealthy, or you're living on retirement income, there's probably no need to spend money on insurance premiums. Invest it elsewhere. There are, however, several exceptions. If you are a widow with no children or your children are on their own yet you are helping a less fortunate sibling, or if your parents require your financial help, you'll want to have insurance to take care of those you are helping should you die first. Another exception: if your estate is worth more than $1 million, it will be subject to federal estate taxes. You may want to have enough insurance to cover the IRS bill; otherwise your heirs may have to liquidate your assets to pay the taxes. (This is a topic to discuss in detail with your lawyer or accountant.)

IF YOU HAVE YOUNG CHILDREN

Coverage is critical if you have dependent children. How much is determined by how many children you have, how old they are, and what other sources of income they have, such as a trust fund or insurance left by their father. The rule of thumb is that insurance should cover six to eight times your annual salary. Or, figure out how much your dependents will need to cover their education bills and to pay off any mortgage and other major loans that you currently have.

> $TIP: You'll find a helpful calculator at http://money. cnn.com/pf/insurance.

Life insurance comes in two basic types: _term_ and _cash value life insurance_. Cash value insurance is also called permanent insurance. With both, the younger you are when you take out a policy, the cheaper it will be.

TERM LIFE INSURANCE

The least expensive type of coverage (and the easiest to buy and the type I generally recommend) is term insurance. It:

- Provides only life insurance—that is, it pays a specific death benefit to your beneficiary provided you die during the term covered. (If you have not kept your policy up to date, there is no payout.)

- Provides coverage only for a specific time or "term" just as the name indicates, usually 1, 5, 10, or 20 years.

- Has absolutely no savings feature—that is, no cash value and therefore you cannot borrow against it.

- Has an annual renewable premium that is based on your age, health, and other statistics. According to ReliaQuote at Insurance. com, if you are 40 years old and in good health, a 15-year policy for $100,000 will probably cost you $150 a year in premiums.

- Must be renewed at the end of every term, with the premium increasing each term.

- May, in some cases, be renewable at the end of the term without a medical exam.

- May, in some cases, be converted. Although there is no cash buildup—that is, no savings—inside a term policy, you can buy a "convertible" term policy that can be rolled over, for a higher premium, into permanent insurance, without a medical exam.

A variation on the theme is level term insurance, meaning your premium payments are fixed for the entire term. Your premium will be higher than with renewable term, but it won't rise during the term and you may save money over a longer period of time. Level term is usually purchased when the need for coverage is for a specific period, say until your children have completed college.

For example, a one-year renewable term offers guaranteed coverage up until a certain age, often 75, regardless of your health. The premium rises annually.

On the other hand, a level term policy typically guarantees a fixed premium for 10 to 30 years. It costs more than one-year term during the beginning years but less in the later years. Over the entire period, it's usually cheaper than a one-year renewable policy.

CASH VALUE LIFE INSURANCE

The other type of life insurance is cash value or permanent insurance. Part insurance and part investment, it is called permanent because as long as you pay your premiums it provides coverage. It does not end on a certain date as does term insurance. And unlike term, it has a tax-deferred savings feature, the premiums are generally fixed, and they do not increase with age.

During the early years, the premium exceeds the insurance company's estimated cost of insuring your life. Then after several years, the surplus and interest are channeled into a tax-deferred savings-like fund. The fund is usually in conservative long-term bonds and mortgages and/or blue chip stocks. If you cancel your policy, you receive the cash value back in a lump sum, minus administrative costs and any agent's commission.

One of the few advantages cash value or permanent has over term is that you can borrow from your cash reserve, typically at low rates. You don't have to pay back the loan, then the amount due will be subtracted from the death benefit.

Within this broad category there are four basic types of coverage: whole life, universal life, variable life, and variable universal.

With whole life, also called ordinary or straight life, the premiums remain the same for the entire life of the policy. Part of the premium pays for the fixed death benefit and part is invested and earns a fixed rate of interest. The policy remains in place until you die, at which time the company pays a predetermined

WHEN YOU'RE TOO OLD FOR TERM INSURANCE

It's easy for women to hang on to term insurance long after it's smart. True, it provides a lump sum upon death, but it has no investment value. And the premiums begin to rise rapidly when you hit midlife. For example, State Farm Insurance charges a nonsmoking female in good health about $385 per year for a $100,000 policy at age 50. When she hits 60, the cost is $742 and at age 70, it's not even available. Consider giving up term when:

- You have educated your children

- You have paid off your mortgage

- You have become independently wealthy

- You have a sizable pension

- You are retired

death benefit to the beneficiary. Some whole life policies allow you to make payments for a set number of years (often seven) and then borrow against the accumulated cash value to pay for future premiums.

Universal life is popular because of its flexible features. The death benefit can be increased or decreased after the policy is in effect. You can use the money in your cash buildup to meet premium payments. You can cash in the policy at any time and get back most of your savings. You may be able to designate how much you want to go into insurance and how much into savings. The rate of return is variable; it is typically tied to an index, such as the Treasury bill rate. Rates generally are guaranteed for one year, but, when changed, will not fall below the minimum stated in the policy, which, for example, is about 4% in a GE Universal Life policy.

A variable life policy is designed basically for investment growth. The cash portion is invested in mutual funds that you select from a menu of funds. Consequently, both the death benefit and the cash value vary, based on how successfully your cash reserve is invested. Most policies guarantee that the death benefit will not fall below a specified minimum.

A variable universal policy combines the premium and death benefit flexibility of universal life with the investment flexibility and risk of variable life. You choose your premium and death benefit, and the death benefit and cash value fluctuate according to the performance of the funds.

Caution: Because variable life and variable universal life policyholders assume most of the investment risk involved, these policies are considered securities contracts and must be registered with the SEC.

BOTTOM LINE

Because the purpose of life insurance is to protect your heirs or beneficiaries and not to build your savings account or investment portfolio, I recommend term insurance rather than cash value. Not only is term considerably less expensive, it is easier to purchase. Granted, cash value policies offer tax-deferred savings, but the rates are often unimpressive. You can build a better tax-deferred account through your IRA, 401(k), or other retirement plan.

For More Help

Life insurance policies are incredibly complex, and it's easy to become confused. Before purchasing coverage, I recommend that you have policies analyzed using the Consumer Federation of America's Life Insurance Rate of Return Analysis Service. It estimates investment returns on any cash value life policy. The cost for the analysis is $50 for the first and $35 for each additional policy submitted at the same time. Contact CFA at 603-224-2805 or www.consumerfed. org/backpage/evaluate_insurance_policy.html.

Buy life insurance only from a company that is rated A or above. See page 88 for information on how to find ratings.

Buy direct or from low-load companies. You will save money if you don't go through an agent. Ameritas (800-552-3553 or www. ameritasdirect.com), for example, sells directly to the public.

Use a quote service. The following three services will send you the five (sometimes more) policies that match your needs and price range. You will be asked your age, general health status, ZIP code, whether or not you smoke, and similar details.

- SelectQuote: 800-343-1985 or www.selectquote.com

- TermQuote: 800-444-8376 or www.termquote.com (specializes in term insurance)

- QuoteSmith Corp.: 800-556-9393 or quotesmith.com

Use an agent. If you wish to use an agent, look for one that has specific credentials. The American College in Bryn Mawr, PA, grants two designations—ChFC (Chartered Financial Consultant) and CLU (Chartered Life Underwriter)—to agents who have taken specialized courses in insurance, estate planning, and investments. For names in your area, contact the Society of Financial Service Professionals (866-CH-FCCLU or www.financialpro.org/consumer/referral.chm).

Automobile Insurance

If your husband was the one who took care of your car insurance or if you're buying or selling a car, this section is must reading. Fortunately, automobile insurance is not quite as complicated as life insurance. In fact, all you may need to do is renew your current coverage, letting the company know that your husband died.

An auto insurance policy includes several basic types of coverage:

- Bodily injury liability provides money to pay claims made against you and the cost of your legal defense if your car injures or kills someone.

- Property damage liability provides money to pay claims and defense costs if your car damages the property of others.

    Note: You want to have enough bodily injury liability to cover your assets—better yet, double your assets. The minimum I recommend is $300,000 for bodily injury suffered by one person in each accident, $500,000 for injuries suffered by all persons in the same accident, and $100,000 for damage to property. On your policy, this will be written as 300/500/100.

- Medical payments pays medical expenses resulting from accidental injuries to you and the passengers in your car without regard as to who caused the accident. It also covers you when riding in someone else's car or when you are a pedestrian.

    $TIP: If you have other medical insurance, you may not need this medical coverage.

- Uninsured motorists pays for injuries caused by an uninsured or a hit-and-run driver.

    Note: You should have at least $100,000 per person, $300,000 per accident, and $50,000 property damage. On your policy, this will be written as 100/300/50.

- Collision insurance pays for damage to your car resulting from a collision or from overturning. Although you will be able to collect no matter who caused the accident, the coverage generally does not pay more than the current value of the car.

- Comprehensive physical damage pays for damages when your car is stolen or damaged by fire, flooding, hail, or other perils. It also covers you against theft, vandalism, and damage by falling objects.

12 WAYS TO KEEP INSURANCE PREMIUMS DOWN

1. Comparison shop. You can save hundreds of dollars (sometimes thousands, depending on the number of cars and drivers in your family) by making a few phone calls or checking websites. Take the time to call at least three local agents for quotes and then go to:

- Progressive Insurance: 800-PROGRESSIVE or www.progressive.com
- Insure: www.insure.com
- Insurance Quotes: www.insweb.com

2. Take the highest deductibles possible. To keep insurance premiums low and eliminate the need to file for small losses, take the highest deductibles you can. On an auto policy, there are two deductibles: collision and comprehensive. With both, you want just enough to cover the losses you cannot afford. Raising deductibles to $500 or $1,000 will cut as much as 40% from collision and comprehensive insurance bills.

3. Skip some coverage. If you drive an old clunker, you could drop the collision coverage. Insurers will not pay out more than a vehicle's book value, even if it's totally ruined in an accident. So never pay more in collision insurance premiums than your car is worth.

4. Get group rates. You may be able to insure your car through your employer. Or, if you are or were in the armed forces, call USAA (800-531-8080 or www.usaa.com).

5. Buy a used car. It will cost significantly less to insure—up to 30% in some cases.

> **$TIP:** Don't buy a lemon. Cars that were declared lemons and then repurchased by car manufacturers are often resold in used car lots. Before buying a used car, check its Vehicle Identification Number (VIN). You can do so at www.autocheck.com or www.carfax.com. Both sites allow you to review the car's history and will reveal odometer discrepancies. The fee is about $15/car.

6. Talk to an auto mechanic. They sometimes know which insurance companies are the best to deal with.

> **$TIP:** If you don't have a mechanic, head for an inspection center that is certified by the Car Care Council (www.carcarecouncil.com). This organization educates motorists on car maintenance and safety.

7. Drive a low-profile car. The hot models that thieves favor plus all sports cars and luxury models cost more to insure than the more pedestrian models.

> **$TIP:** The National Insurance Crime Bureau compiles a top-ten stolen cars list each year. Among the models that appear on this list are the Toyota Camry, Honda Accord, Jeep Cherokee, Grand Cherokee, and Ford Taurus. For more information on vehicles with good, mediocre, and poor ratings for insurance losses and thefts, log on to www.hwysafety.org/vehicle_ratings.htm.

8. Just say no to unnecessary options. They may duplicate protection you already have such as life insurance, disability, cover-

age for towing, and theft insurance. Your homeowner's policy, for example, may cover the contents of your car that are stolen.

9. Don't always file claims. File claims only if there's a chance someone has been hurt. It's too expensive to file for damage under a few hundred dollars and it may drive up your rates.

10. Pay premiums annually. Installment plans are convenient but wind up costing you more because of the interest or service fees added on.

11. Know the rules about family and friends. Teenagers are not automatically covered when they get their drivers license. The insurance carrier must be notified. If you fail to do so and your child is in an accident, your coverage could be dropped.

Generally, you are insured when you drive another person's car but not if they are considered "regularly available." For example, if your college student has regular access to a roommate's car, he or she may not be covered by the roommate's policy. Avoid regularly sharing cars or if you do, check with your insurer.

12. Speak up for discounts. Make sure you tell the insurance company about any of the following that apply; they may reduce your premium. For example, if you don't smoke, you will pay 10% to 25% less than a smoker.

☐ Driver is a nonsmoker

☐ Driver is a nondrinker

☐ Driver is a graduate of a driver education program

☐ Driver is a student with good grades

☐ Driver has accident-free record

☐ Driver is in a car pool

☐ Driver insures more than one car with the insurance company

☐ Driver has other insurance with the company

☐ Driver is a member of a preferred profession, such as a doctor or lawyer

☐ Driver is a member of AARP

- [ ] Driver is over age 50
- [ ] Car has been driven less than 7,500 miles per year
- [ ] Car has an ignition cutoff system
- [ ] Car has airbags
- [ ] Car has a hood-locking device
- [ ] Car has a wheel-locking device
- [ ] Car has a security alarm

Some insurance companies allow their customers to have a one-time, no-fault accident without increasing the premium. Although it's not industry wide, find out if your company has this "forgiveness" practice. If not, consider changing insurers. Companies that forgive first-time accidents may ask that you meet certain requirements. At USAA, for example, you must have a clear driving record and have been insured with the company for six years. State Farm's "forgive the first accident" policy is for those who have been insured by the company for at least nine years. The Hartford will forgive first accidents if the customer causes less than $1,000 in property damage.

DRIVE A SAFE CAR

Safe cars are not just safe, they are less expensive to insure. The Insurance Institute for Highway Safety (www.highwaysafety.org) tests hundreds of models every year to determine which ones offer the best protection in collisions. Among these models are the Honda Civic, Volkswagen New Beetle, Toyota Camry, Buick LeSabre, Pontiac Bonneville, Cadillac Seville, Ford Windstar, and Lexus RX 300. Check the website for a complete listing.

A WINTER CHECKUP

As you face the first winter without your husband, you will need to arrange a checkup for your car to make sure it is ready for freezing weather, sleet, and snow. According to *Motor Week* magazine, the seven things you should check are:

1. The battery. Have a qualified technician do a heavy-load test, especially if your car still has its original battery and it is three years old, or older.

2. The radiator. Make certain there's adequate antifreeze/coolant.

3. The tires. The more worn your tires are, the less traction you'll have in heavy snow or on icy roads.

4. The brakes. Have a good repairperson make sure your brakes are in A-1 condition.

5. Window wipers. Buy new wiper blades so that you'll be protected against snow and ice on your windshield.

6. Windshield washer fluid. Your windshield washer fluid should have antifreeze in it.

7. Door locks. Spray graphite lubricant in all door locks.

SELLING YOUR WHEELS

If you're trying to decide if it's time to trade in your 4 x 4 or Caddy that zigs, have the car inspected by an independent mechanic whom you trust. Get a written estimate of necessary repairs. The three common signs that problems may be too expensive to repair are:

1. Blue smoke indicates serious valve trouble

2. Knocking may mean worn bearings

3. Rust, if it's major, can weaken the structure; smaller spots of rust also reduce the car's value

After you get a mechanic's opinion, find out how much your car is worth using the *Kelley Blue Book* (www.kbb.com), then deduct the cost of repair from the book value. If the cost is significantly more than the book value, you probably should sell the car or trade it in. (See Chapter 14 for tips on selling or donating a car to charity.)

LOANING OUT YOUR CAR

Humorist, author, and mother and grandmother of many drivers Erma Bombeck offered this advice: "Never lend your car to anyone to whom you have given birth." Nor should you give your car to anyone else unless you know for a fact that he or she:

☐ Has a valid drivers license   ☐ Does not drink and drive

☐ Is covered by insurance   ☐ Does not do drugs and drive

☐ Is a safe driver   ☐ Does not yak on a cell phone and drive

In some instances, letting certain people drive your car may invalidate the insurance coverage normally afforded to occasional drivers.

For More Help

Nine Ways to Lower Your Automobile Insurance Costs and many other helpful publications are free from the National Insurance Consumer Helpline (800-942-4242 or www.iii.org).

Homeowner's and Renter's Insurance

Most likely, you and your husband had a homeowner's policy or, if you rented, renter's insurance. If so, set aside time to review it within the next few weeks and then make it a practice of going over it on an annual basis.

Homeowner's policies generally provide a "package" of insurance, including money to cover:

• Repairs or replacement for your house, furniture, and other personal items

- Claims and lawsuits against you and members of your household for injury or property damage you cause

- Additional living expenses should damage to your home force you to live temporarily in a hotel and eat in restaurants

There are several types, ranging from basic to comprehensive. Basic insures your home against fire, lightning, theft, windstorms, hail, explosion, smoke, and other threats. The most comprehensive form covers what is known as the "18 perils."

THE STRUCTURE

Your physical structure should be insured for 100% of the replacement value. Don't go by the amount your mortgage lender requires. The bank's only concern is that it will be covered for the balance due on your mortgage.

You want enough money to rebuild your house at current prices should it be destroyed. Don't confuse that with what your house would sell for in today's market. It's the rebuilding figure that you want. An insurance representative or a professional appraiser can help you determine this dollar amount.

If you've lived in your house or condo for many years, unless you've updated your coverage, your policy may no longer be adequate enough to replace the building should it be severely damaged or destroyed. I recommend adding an inflation _rider_ that will automatically increase coverage at each renewal date in order to keep pace with current construction costs in your area.

An even better solution (if it's available) is guaranteed full replacement coverage so that your insurer will pay whatever it costs to rebuild your house. This type of policy costs about 10% more than one with a dollar cap.

FLOOD INSURANCE

Flood damage is _not_ covered by homeowner's insurance. Coverage must be purchased separately. You may not think you're a likely candidate for flooding yet more than 25% of flood claims come from areas not prone to flooding, due to hurricanes, high tides, and other disasters that damage inland areas. If you live near a coast, river, lake, creek, golf course pond, or a low-lying area, you should have coverage. It averages about $400 per year. Not all insurance companies sell flood insurance. To find one that does, get in touch with the Federal Emergency Management Agency (FEMA) at 800-427-4661 or www.fema.gov/nfip.

YOUR POSSESSIONS

Your policy should also have replacement cost coverage for your personal property. If you have a flood or fire and your living room furniture is destroyed, the insurance company will pay you enough money to buy new furniture that is comparable to the pieces that were lost.

Avoid a policy that covers items for their actual cash value, which is their original cost minus an amount subtracted for _depreciation,_ or wear and tear.

INVENTORIES AND DOCUMENTATION

In order to document the replacement cost of items, you need to have an up-to-date household inventory. Set aside a Saturday and take snapshots or a video of all your possessions. Don't forget the basement, attic, garage, or an off-site storage unit. Note each item's condition and age. Record serial numbers for such items as computers, TVs, VCRs, and so on, and back up your visual inventory with as many sales receipts as you can locate. Then, make a copy of the pictures and receipts, keeping one set in your safe deposit box and the other in a separate place, ideally with someone who lives out of town.

Update your inventory when you acquire or sell possessions or give them away.

Once again, make sure your coverage is for replacement costs and not actual cash value.

INSURING VALUABLES

In a standard policy, jewelry, silverware, and watches are typically covered up to a stated maximum—often $2,000 to $3,000. If you

TEN WAYS TO SAVE MONEY ON HOMEOWNER'S INSURANCE

1. Buy home and auto policies from the same company. Typically you'll get a 5% to 20% discount.

2. Ask about savings for seniors. If you are 55 and retired, you may qualify for a 10% discount.

3. Insure only your home. The land it sits on is not at risk for theft, vandalism, or fire.

4. Install security. Smoke detectors, burglar alarms, or deadbolt locks may give you a 5% discount.

5. Don't smoke. Your costs will drop significantly.

6. Think about your pets. Dogs considered dangerous, such as pit bulls, rottweilers, and German shepherds, more often than not boost premiums.

7. Remain loyal. Some insurers offer a 5% discount if you stay with them three to five years, and more for longer stays.

8. Raise your annual deductible. You can cut your premium up to 15% by raising the amount you agree to pay out of pocket before any insurance reimbursement kicks in.

9. Speak up if you have a new house. Some companies lower premiums by 5% to 20% for those whose homes are less than five years old.

10. Skip floaters you no longer need. If you donated your fabulous fur to a charity, or you gave your daughter your silver tea set, cancel your floater.

have family heirlooms, valuable artwork, antiques, jewelry, or furs, you should have a separate _floater_ providing extra coverage for certain stated valuables. Unless you've just purchased these items and have the sale receipts, arrange for a professional to appraise them. For names of appraisers contact:

- American Society of Appraisers: 703-478-2228 or www. appraisers.org

- Appraisers Association of America: 212-889-5404 or www. appraisersassoc.org

Make certain you have an *all-risk insurance coverage* in your floater so you will be reimbursed no matter how your valuables were lost. A typical floater costs an additional $10.20 per $1,000 worth of jewelry. For collectibles it's about $4.50 per $1,000 worth of coverage. Furniture and art floaters range from about 90 cents to $4 per $1,000.

OFFICE EQUIPMENT

If you have a computer, fax, printer, or other office equipment in a home-based office, talk to your agent about insuring them separately, perhaps through a home office rider.

Liability Insurance

This type of coverage is usually purchased in conjunction with auto or homeowner's insurance. You've probably heard it referred to as an "umbrella policy." It provides protection when you are sued—if someone slips on your sidewalk and is hurt, for example. At a minimum, you should have $1 million worth of coverage.

For More Help

The National Insurance Consumer Helpline, 800-942-4242, will answer questions from 8:00 A.M. to 8:00 P.M. ET.

Home Insurance Basics and other useful publications are free from the Insurance Information Institute (www.iii.org).

About Choosing an Insurance Agent, Life Advice (800-MET-LIFE or www.lifeadvice.com)

Investing and Estate Planning

Chapter Ten

YOUR TEAM OF EXPERTS

Where large sums of money are concerned, it is advisable to trust nobody.

—AGATHA CHRISTIE

I don't fully agree with Agatha Christie's comment that one should trust nobody where money is concerned, but she was indeed right to be concerned. It is essential that as a widow you find honorable, intelligent, and trustworthy people to advise you about all things financial—stocks, bonds, real estate, insurance, savings, taxes, and estate planning.

The accountant, agent, attorney, broker, or financial planner you select can make the difference between you being a success and failure, and between you being in charge of your money or merely letting someone else, often a stranger, pull the strings.

Even if your husband left you very well off, it is up to you to safeguard those assets and to help them grow to ensure a comfortable retirement for yourself and an enriching life and first-rate education for your children.

Caution: I want you to know up front that *there are exceptions to every bit of advice that appears in this chapter.* My general information and guidelines will help you assemble a good team but, in the last analysis, it comes down to the individual expert—if he or she is topnotch and will work hard for you.

Having said that, let's look at the overall scene.

Sit Tight

The advice I gave you about housing—don't make major moves during the first months after your husband's death—applies to money matters as well. You're going through a trying time during which it's difficult to know what to deal with first. And until you feel comfortable making major decisions, don't. Focus instead on the three initial tasks we reviewed at the beginning of the book: settle your husband's estate, pay your bills on time, and set up a working budget.

You can put off other money issues for 6 to 12 months. During that time, if you have money coming in from an insurance policy or other sources, stash it temporarily in a money market fund, bank CD, or short-term U.S. Treasuries (see Chapter 11 for details about these and other types of investments) where it will be safe, earning a respectable interest rate. In the long term, however, you must diversify as these types of investments are terribly conservative.

Many widows find that from the day their spouse dies and for months afterward, they are inundated with advice. Some of it, of course, is well-meaning, coming from people who really care. But much of it also comes from those looking for business, which may not be right for you.

Your own children may also be pushing you in the wrong direction. It's not unusual for an adult son or daughter to urge Mom to sell her house right away and move in to perhaps help take care of the grandchildren. This often turns out to be a mistake. Many widows, initially feeling distraught, think they can't afford to keep their house when in fact they have sufficient income to stay put. Children may see only one tiny piece of your total financial picture. It is essential that *you* learn to make decisions based on all the facts.

Picking Members of Your Team

Once you are ready to make a move, to find professionals to help you, begin in the usual manner—ask around. Word-of-mouth recommendations are the best way to begin a search for just about anyone—a lawyer, accountant, travel agent, or doctor. Talk only to intelligent members of your family and your brightest friends and colleagues. Note my emphasis on "intelligent" and "bright." Skip over those who are not financially savvy and instead consult only with people you know have been successful. If you already have an attorney or accountant whom you trust, ask him or her for names. If your husband's advisers did a superb job, you can stick with them, but if you have any doubts, don't. If you receive pressure from your brother-in-law the stockbroker, resist, unless he's a real winner.

Then you absolutely must conduct one-on-one interviews, even if your recommendations are coming from the head of the Federal Reserve Board. Just because someone comes with high praise doesn't mean that person is right for you. It is essential that you deal only with those experts with whom you feel at ease discussing all aspects of your financial life. And that's something you won't know until you judge for yourself.

A good financial expert will spend an hour or so with you (for free) at an initial meeting, telling you what to expect by way of services and asking about your circumstances. The two of you should be looking for a good fit and, on your part, a feeling of trust.

HOW THEY MAKE A LIVING

Before you interview the first candidate for your financial team, I want you to understand that these pros are in business to make money not friends—something women often forget about. Financial planners, advisers, accountants, attorneys, and stockbrokers earn a living in one of several ways:

- They earn a commission based on selling financial products—stocks, bonds, annuities, insurance policies, mutual funds, and so on

- They charge an hourly fee

- They charge a percentage based on the assets you are investing or the amount of money they are managing

Don't be shy about asking how someone is paid. It's money out of your pocket and you have a right to know how much will be going for fees and commissions.

THE KEY PLAYERS

Although planning your financial life is up to you and you alone, you don't have to actually go it alone. Here are the key players:

Financial Planner A good financial planner takes a holistic approach, looking at your overall situation—your net worth, your monthly income, and your expenses as well as your financial goals, such as how to pay for college, buy a house, go back to school, pay off the mortgage, or retire. Then, together, you can work out a strategy to meet those goals. A financial planner will draw up a plan, a comprehensive road map, covering your savings, taxes, investments, insurance needs, and estate planning. The plan should spell out what you need to do in each of these areas and indicate how often you will meet—probably twice a year—to review what has taken place and to make necessary changes.

I think most women are best off with a fee-only planner who is paid solely for his or her advice. The up-front fee, may be a percentage of your portfolio, a per-hour fee, or a flat fee for an entire plan. Fee-only planners do not make commissions from any investments or insurance products they may recommend, which gives them a great deal of independence and leeway in determining what's best for you. It also does away with the conflict of interest involved in recommending an investment that pays the planner a fee or commission.

For a list of fee-only planners in your area, contact the National Association of Personal Financial Advisers (888-FEE-ONLY or www.napfa.org).

A fee-plus-commission-based planner likewise offers financial advice but can also sell products, including insurance and mutual funds. This type of planner charges a set fee and also earns commissions on the investments or products recommended. In that respect, they are like insurance agents and stockbrokers. Although a commission-based planner offers the convenience of a one-stop service, you must question how objective this type of planner can be. For example, he or she may be able to sell you only certain mutual funds rather than being able to select from a wider universe. That doesn't mean the funds will be duds, but it is possible that with some fee-plus-commission-based planners there could be a conflict of interest.

Within the overall group of financial planners, select one that has one of the following professional designations. Although the designation does not automatically mean the planner is a genius, it does indicate that the person has completed a fairly difficult course of study, which demonstrates a level of intelligence. I think it also indicates seriousness about the work.

- Certified Financial Planner (CFP). A CFP must complete a tough certification exam and then finish 30 hours of continuing education every two years. The license is awarded by the Certified Planning Board of Standards for the Denver-based Institute of Financial Planners. The Board (888-CFP-MARK or cfp-board.org) will tell you if a CFP has ever been disciplined. For a list of CFPs in your area, contact the Financial Planning Association (800-647-6340 or www.fpanet.org). *Note:* The CFP designation can be revoked by the CFP Board of Standards, an ethical oversight committee. This occurs when the planner breaches the code of conduct.

- Chartered Financial Consultant (ChFC). A ChFC has finished a ten-course program run by the American College and must have at least three years experience. For the names of ChFCs in your area, contact the American Society of CLU and ChFC (800-392-6900 or www.agents-online.com/ASCLU/index.html).

- Personal Financial Specialist (PFS). This is a certified public accountant who is also trained in personal finance and has passed a six-hour test and had at least three years of experience in financial planning. For a list of CPAs with the PFS designation, contact the American Institute of Certified Public Accountants (888-999-9256 or www.cpapfs.org).

Before you hire a financial planner, whether or not he or she has one of the above designations, check with the North American Securities Administrators Association (202-737-0900 or www.nasaa.org) to determine if any lawsuits or complaints have been filed against that person.

The Securities and Exchange Commission (800-SEC-0330 or www.sec.gov/investor/brokers.htm) has information on registered investment advisory firms. Called the Investment Adviser Public Disclosure (ADV) form, it contains information about a firm and its business operations as well as disclosure about certain disciplinary events involving the firm and its key personnel. *Note:* The SEC website also has excellent information about interviewing and selecting an adviser.

Stockbroker If you own individual stocks or bonds and other securities that sell on the open market or wish to, you will need a stockbroker to handle the transactions. Stockbrokers earn a commission on each investment you buy or sell. *Note:* There are a handful of companies that sell their stock directly to investors, thus bypassing brokers.

There are two types of brokers: full service and discount. Both must be employed by a member firm of the National Association of Security Dealers (NASD) and pass a comprehensive exam called a Series 7. Only upon successful completion of the exam is the broker registered and allowed to buy and sell securities for customers.

A full-service broker charges higher commissions than a discount broker, but he in turn offers investment advice. He will tell you which stocks to buy and help you work out both long- and short-term strategies. If he is truly professional, he will continually monitor your holdings, send you research reports, and advise you on when to sell a security.

Some firms promote their reps as financial advisers or financial consultants. Merrill Lynch, for example, gives brokers a three-year course that includes earning the CPF designation. However, according to a recent *BusinessWeek* report, only 1,000 of Merrill's 13,400 U.S. brokers have earned the CFP mark.

Discount brokers, such as Quick & Reilly and Charles Schwab, charge less but also offer less. Their fees can be as much as 70%

lower than those of a full-service broker. Discounters do not give individual advice about what to buy or sell, although some firms do make research available.

If you are savvy about investing, you can reduce your commissions even more by executing your own trades over the Internet with an online broker. In 1995, there were only 12 such firms. Now there are a great many including a number of well-known firms such as Ameritrade, Fidelity, Schwab, ScottTrade, and E*Trade.

Before opening an online account, spend some time studying the information offered by Gomez Advisers (www.gomez.com). This service rates e-brokers in terms of customer support, speed, accuracy, objectives, and costs.

Whether you opt for a full-service broker, a discount broker, or an online broker, you must first contact the National Association of Securities Dealers Regulation (800-289-9999 or www.nasdr.com) to find out if a broker is licensed to operate in your state and if any complaints or disciplinary actions have been filed against him. This group maintains a huge database known as the Central Registration Depository (CRD). It contains a broker's employment history for the past ten years, certain felonies and misdemeanors, bankruptcies or outstanding liens, investment-related disciplinary actions, consumer complaints alleging fraud or losses of $10,000 or more, and consumers complaints that were settled for at least $5,000.

NASD will give you an abbreviated report. For the full report, contact your state securities commission.

INSURANCE AGENT

Agents come in two types: exclusive agents who represent just one insurance company and independent agents who represent several companies. Exclusive agents sometimes can get you a better price because their commissions are lower, but the independents can obviously quote you rates from a number of different insurers.

Note: You'll also find a number of sources you can use for making quick comparisons of rates in Chapter 9.

You can also buy insurance directly from some companies. And as you know from Chapter 9, most employers and many professional associations offer coverage to individuals at group rates. Credit unions do likewise. Contact the Credit Union National Association (800-358-5710 or www.cuna.org) to find one you can join.

ATTORNEY

You'll find that attorneys, like doctors, have become more and more specialized. Although there are many who still have a general practice, most are experts in one or two of these areas: estate planning, real estate, taxes, marriage and divorce, patents, elder law, and personal finance and debt. If your legal issues are fairly simple and straightforward, there's no reason why you can't use a general practitioner. For complex matters, it's wise to use a specialist.

The way attorneys invoice clients can be confusing. When interviewing a prospective attorney, don't be shy; ask how you will be billed and what is included—long-distance phone calls, photocopying, mailing, messenger service, and so on. You may be asked for a retainer—that is, money up front. You may be charged by the hour or by the project, although some firms have fixed fees for certain tasks, such as writing a will, revising a will, or filing incorporation papers. An attorney may also use the contingency fee method in which case the dollar amount is contingent upon the results of the case. In other words, the attorney accepts a percentage of the money the client wins when the case is settled. In large firms, partners charge considerably more than associates. Therefore, unless you have a particularly difficult case, you may not need to hire the top gun.

Certification A growing number of states certify attorneys who specialize in particular areas. The certification requirements vary from state to state but most include continuing education, passing tough written exams, and a peer review. Among the areas the American Bar Association has certification programs in are business and consumer bankruptcy, civil and criminal trial advocacy, estate planning, elder law, and professional liability. For more information on state and private certification programs, contact the American Bar Association's

SHOULD YOU USE A DISCOUNT BROKER?

YES, if:

- You like to select your own stocks and bonds

- You belong to an investment club

- You have inherited a few shares you want to sell

- You have time to follow the market

- You subscribe to an investment service

- You follow technical indicators

- You read or listen to the market news on a regular basis

- You trade frequently

- You are not afraid to make mistakes

NO, if:

- You cannot decide what to buy and sell

- You require investment advice

- You are too busy to follow the market

- You are nervous about things financial

- You are inexperienced

Standing Committee on Specialization (312-988-6000 or www.abanet.org/legalservices/specialization).

For help in finding an attorney in your area, contact your local bar association. If you don't find the number in the local phone directory, call the ABA (312-988-5000). Another useful source with information on finding and hiring an attorney is Find Legal Help (www.FindLegalHelp.org), an online service sponsored by the ABA.

You can also refer to the *Martindale-Hubbell Law Directory,* available at most libraries and online at www.martindalehubbell.com. It gives information on each lawyer's specialties, education, experience, and general background.

TAX PREPARER

Many women find they are able to prepare their own tax return; provided it is relatively simple. But for the year in which your husband died (or any time you have a complicated tax situation), you would be well advised to get professional help. There are four general categories of tax preparers:

1. Commercial preparers. This is the most basic and the broadest group. It includes the one-person or Mom-and-Pop-type operation—those preparers who set up shop during tax season and then disappear until next year—as well as large, well-known firms, such as H&R Block. Most commercial preparers who accept walk-in clients do not specialize in complicated returns and do not handle IRS audits.

If you have a simple return but would feel more comfortable with someone else filling out the forms, this is the right place to be. But make sure the firm or person you use is in business 12 months a year—in other words, it doesn't close up shop on April 16. Figure on paying about $100.

2. Enrolled agents. These preparers—there are about 9,600 of them nationwide—are more expensive, more sophisticated, and have more expertise than most commercial preparers. In fact, they are licensed by the Treasury Department to represent taxpayers before the IRS. An enrolled agent must have passed a rigorous two-day written exam, administered by the IRS, and/or had at least five years' continuous employment with the IRS in a tax-related job. EAs are also required to take 24 hours of continuing professional education each year to keep their designation.

EAs, whose rates are more than those of commercial preparers and less than those of CPAs, figure $250 to $300 for an itemized return with some additional work, such as out-of-state returns. They almost always work exclusively in the world of taxes and therefore tend to be up to date on all the ramifications of the tax code.

To find an EA in your area, contact the National Association of Enrolled Agents (800-424-4339 or www.naea.org).

3. Certified public accountants. CPAs are college grads and are licensed by the state. Prior to licensing, they must pass a rigorous

---

WHY YOU MIGHT NEED A TAX PREPARER

If, during the calendar year, any of the following happened to you, I assure you that your return will be particularly complicated:

- Your husband died
- You bought or sold a house
- You started your own business
- You folded a business
- You operated a home office
- You retired
- You became a day trader
- You collected rental or royalty income
- You were a trustee, executor, legal guardian, or conservator
- You took a lump-sum payment from a retirement plan

- You moved to a new state
- Your work required you to travel outside the United States
- You lost property in a flood, earthquake, or hurricane
- Your income level changed dramatically
- You remarried
- You had a baby
- You adopted a child
- You came into an inheritance

two-and-a-half-day exam and have worked under supervision for two years. In most states they must take 40 hours of continuing education courses every year. CPAs, like EAs, can represent taxpayers before the IRS.

CPAs charge anywhere from several hundred dollars to more than $1,000 depending upon the complexity of the return.

To find a CPA in your area, get in touch with the American Institute of Certified Public Accountants (212-596-6200 or www.aicpa.org).

Another nationwide source is the CPA Directory (800-CPA-DIRECT or www.cpadirectory.com). You'll also find the financial calculators, tax tips, and legislative updates on the website very useful.

4. Tax attorneys. These lawyers may or may not be tax preparers. They serve as legal advisers, helping those with complicated tax and estate situations. If you're in a very high-income bracket and have an unusual personal- or business-related tax life, you may wish to consult with one. Be prepared to pay several hundred dollars an hour.

Interviewing Tips

Now that you've had time to think about who should be on your financial team of experts, your next step is to begin interviewing the candidates. This should not be a long-distance, email-only relationship.

Avoid the temptation to sign up with the first financial planner, accountant, or lawyer you speak with. I recommend that you schedule interviews with at least three candidates. By the time you wind up the third interview, you will have a good idea of which one to use. Go to each meeting prepared with a set of standard questions and a notebook. Write down the answers (it's easy to forget them or get confused later on) and compare how each potential adviser answered your queries.

THE ESSENTIAL QUESTIONS TO ASK

Here are the key questions to ask of any financial adviser. Adapt them to accommodate your particular situation.

1. How long have you been in this business? With this firm? Do you belong to any professional organizations? Do you take continuing education classes?

2. Where were you trained?

3. Do you have any specialties?

4. What percentage of your clients are widows?

5. Will you give me three references? (Take the time to call each reference to ask about the candidate's strengths and weaknesses. It can be a pain, but the results can be very revealing.)

6. What will it cost me to use your help? How do you charge? What will that cover and for what time frame? How long do you think this particular project or case will take?

7. What is your greatest strength?

8. What is the minimum amount required to be your client? How large is your average client's portfolio?

9. Do you have other clients like me? Have you handled this particular situation in the past?

10. How often will we meet?

11. Why does my account interest you?

12. Have you ever been suspended or disciplined? (This is the question to which you will want an honest answer, but probably you should get it from other sources.)

Here are further key questions to ask a stockbroker:

1. What do you suggest that I do with my $20,000 (or whatever amount you have)? (Beware of the person who suggests you put it all in one product or security.)

2. What sort of return can I expect from my investment?

3. What research materials do you rely upon? Where do you get your ideas?

4. What stock-picking strategies do you use?

5. What was your best investment last year? Your worst?

6. How do you decide when to sell a stock?

Here are the further key questions to ask an accountant:

1. How large is your firm? (There's nothing wrong with a one-person firm, provided that person can get the work done on time. There's nothing wrong with a huge firm, unless they typically don't handle cases your size.)

2. What other services do you offer? (You might like a firm that will help you with other tasks, such as bookkeeping, preparing reports, preparing balance sheets, and so on. Or, this may not be important to you.)

3. Who will handle my return? (Avoid firms that do returns on a "pool" basis, where several accountants address different aspects of your return.)

4. What research do you use? (You want to work with someone who subscribes to CCH [Commerce Clearing House] or a similar service.)

5. If I'm audited, will you personally represent me before the IRS? (Ideally, you want to work with the professional who will appear for you, so you don't have to be present. And, you don't want the

QUESTIONS MEMBERS OF YOUR TEAM SHOULD ASK YOU

If an adviser is not getting your complete financial picture, you will not be getting the best possible advice. A good adviser will ask about all of these topics. And a good client has all the answers ready.

- ☐ What is your age?
- ☐ How many dependents do you have?
- ☐ What is your net worth?
- ☐ What debts do you have?
- ☐ What is your salaried income?
- ☐ What is your investment income?
- ☐ What benefits or payouts have you received from your husband's estate?
- ☐ What benefits does your employer offer?
- ☐ Are you collecting Social Security? If so, how much?
- ☐ Do you have a will? Power of attorney? Health care proxy?
- ☐ What insurance coverage do you have?
- ☐ How do you feel about taking risks?
- ☐ How much have you saved toward your retirement?
- ☐ Will you be receiving an inheritance?
- ☐ What are your two long-term goals? Two short-term goals?
- ☐ What are you most worried about?
- ☐ What do you want me to do for you?

accountant or EA to send audit work outside the firm. Listen carefully to the answer; you want to hear a resounding yes.)

For More Help

The Financial Planning Resource Kit discusses how to interview and select an ethical financial planner, lists the key questions to ask a planner, and explains how you can assert your rights in the relation-ship. (Much of the material in the kit has been reviewed by the SEC.) It is free from the Certified Financial Planner Board of Standards (888-CFP-MARK or www.CFP.net).

Why Select a Fee-Only Financial Advisor is free from the National Association of Personal Financial Advisors (888-FEE-ONLY or www. napfa.org).

Smart Questions to Ask Your Financial Advisors, by Lynn Brenner (Bloomberg, 1999).

Bottom Line

It's tempting to ignore financial matters, to stay with the status quo. But that can be a huge mistake. As the wonderful wit Will Rogers said, "Even if you're on the right track, you'll get run over if you just sit there."

Chapter Eleven

ESTATE PLANNING

He who knows enough is enough will always have enough.
—LAO TSU

No one likes to sign up for estate planning, except of course estate-planning lawyers. Yet you know, from the trying experience you've just been through, how very, very important it is to carefully arrange what will happen to your money and personal property after you die. Without an estate plan, you could put your family's security in serious jeopardy.

Because you are on your own now, you and only you can make sure your assets are dispersed as you wish, so that your children and other loved ones are properly taken care of and not hit with overwhelming tax bills.

The whole point of estate planning is deciding who should get what. You can leave your property to your heirs and other beneficiaries in one of two ways: outright via your will or in a trust. When you leave your property outright, your say in what happens to it ends when you die. If you leave it in a trust, however, your wishes can be extended according to the instructions you wrote into the trust agreement.

Let's begin with your will.

Writing a Will

A will is a legal document designating the transfer of your property and assets after you die. Wills can usually be written by anyone over the age of 18 and who is mentally sound. This is often referred to as "being of sound mind and memory." Individual states may have additional requirements.

Many women, especially those with small estates, think they don't need a will. Foolish thinking. You may think you don't have much to leave to family and friends, but believe me you do. Even if you don't own your home, you probably have a car, savings account, retirement plan, furniture, and perhaps some jewelry or artwork. Perhaps you have your grandmother's silver or your grandfather's favorite rocking chair. If you die without a will, all assets that do not have a named beneficiary will be divided according to your state's laws. That's certainly not something you want to happen.

A will is also the means through which guardians are named for children. If you are a young widow with dependent children, consult the section on naming guardians in Chapter 12.

You may decide to use the attorney who settled your husband's estate to help you draw up a will or revise your existing one. Because he or she is already familiar with your financial situation and will have most of the details at hand, you will probably pay less than if you hire an attorney new to the situation. On the other hand, if you wish to use a different lawyer, reread the section in Chapter 10 on selecting an attorney that's right for you.

THE BASIC ELEMENTS OF A WILL

Your will should include:

☐ Your name and place of residence

☐ A brief summary of your assets

KINDS OF WILLS

Holographic: A handwritten will and one that is not witnessed. (Not valid in every state.)

Joint: Two wills—the husband's and the wife's—contained in one document.

Living: Tells doctors and hospitals whether or not you wish life support if you are terminally ill or, as a result of an accident or illness, cannot be restored to consciousness. (Not really a will because it does not dispose of property.)

Oral: One that is done verbally with no written version. (Rarely valid.)

Pour-over: Leaves your estate to a trust set up before you die.

Simple: Provides for the distribution of the entire estate to one or more persons or entities so that no part of the estate remains undistributed.

Testamentary-trust: Sets up one or more trusts into which designated portions of your estate are placed after you die.

- ☐ Names of children (and spouse if you remarried) and other beneficiaries, such as relatives, friends, and charities

- ☐ Specific gifts, such as a house, car, boat, art collection, antiques

- ☐ Establishment of trusts, if recommended by your attorney

- ☐ Cancellation of debts owed to you, if you decide to forgive them

- ☐ Name of an executor to manage your estate

- ☐ Name of an alternative executor in case your first choice is unable or unwilling to act

- ☐ Name of guardian for your minor children

☐ Name of an alternative guardian in case your first choice is unable or unwilling to act

☐ Your signature

☐ Signature of witnesses (a beneficiary should not be a witness)

BEFORE MEETING YOUR LAWYER

By doing some homework ahead of time, you can reduce the cost of preparing your will. Here are ten money-savers:

1. Take an inventory of your assets. You may have done this in connection with updating your homeowner's insurance (see Chapter 9). If not, this is a good time to do so. Keep in mind that any assets not mentioned specifically in your will are most likely going to fall under the catchall "residuary clause." The residuary clause typically reads something like, "I give the remainder of my estate to . . ."

2. Organize gifts. If you want children or friends to receive certain items, you need to list them as specific bequests in your will. Many women want to be certain that their jewelry, heirlooms, artwork, and furniture go to individual friends and relatives. Merely telling your daughter that she is to receive your 12-piece place setting of Spode or your best friend that you wish for her to have your William and Mary chest is insufficient. You must designate specific gifts in your will, giving a brief description and location.

3. Decide upon amounts. If you have children, do you want your assets divided equally among them? Or, do you have a child with special needs who will require more financial help than the others? Do you have both adult and minor children?

4. Think about cash bequests and trusts. Are your children or grandchildren (or other beneficiaries) old enough or wise enough to properly handle cash bequests? If not, ask your attorney about setting up a trust with a trustee designated to distribute cash over a certain number of years rather than all at once.

5. Make a list of charities. Do you want to leave money to your favorite charities?

6. Estimate your outstanding debts. Any debts left when you die are typically paid by the estate—and done so *before* your beneficiaries receive their specified inheritance. You may want to clear up existing debts or make provisions for payment of them in your will.

7. Review how your property is titled. Do you have stocks, bonds, or bank accounts held jointly with members of your family? If so, that may alter what you intend to do. Let's say, for example, that according to the terms of your will, your three children are to share equally in your $275,000 estate. You also have a joint savings account with one of the children. The money in that account will go to that child only, making the distribution of all that you own unequal.

8. Consider percentages. Using percentages rather than specific dollar amounts is usually preferable. If, for example, you state that you want to leave $100,000 to each of your three children but your estate, after debt and expenses, totals $275,000, your executor is faced with a sticky problem, a problem that would not arise if you used percentages.

9. Make a list of safe deposit boxes. Note the location and contents of each box, plus the name, address, and phone number of anyone else who has legal access.

10. Draw up a final list of names. Type out the names, addresses, and birth dates of all persons, whether or not related to you, that you expect to name in your will. Make a separate list of your executor(s) and guardians for your minor children.

NAMING AN EXECUTOR

The executor is the person who will oversee the distribution of your assets. Most women choose their husband. However, as a widow, you may wish to name an adult child, a relative, a friend, a financial institution, or an attorney. You should indicate that your estate would pay the executor for this work. If no executor is named, a probate judge will appoint one.

The executor will file the will in probate court, where a judge will decide if it is valid. If it is found to be valid, then your assets will be distributed according to the terms of the will. If your will is found invalid, the assets will be distributed in accordance with state law.

If your estate is large or complex, name an attorney or a financial institution as executor. Financial institutions and estate attorneys are professionals, specialists in the field, not emotionally involved, and readily available. They are also free of any conflict of interest with members of your family.

A family member or friend would be less expensive but he or she may not truly understand estate plans and trusts. If this person is too close to your family, he or she may not act 100% impartially, especially if he is in disagreement with some aspect of your wishes. And, of course, an individual could die or be too ill to undertake the task.

NAMING BENEFICIARIES

Be sure to state the full name and address of all your beneficiaries. You also want to note the person's relationship to you, such as child, brother, cousin, friend, or neighbor. The clearer you are, the less likely your will may be challenged.

SIGNING THE WILL

State rules require that you sign the will in front of witnesses. The number of witnesses varies by state; most require at least two. And, just to repeat: a witness should never be a beneficiary named in the will.

UPDATING YOUR WILL

You'll need to change certain parts of your will when life changes—for example, when you remarry, have a grandchild, move to a different state, come into an inheritance, start earning significantly more money, or someone mentioned in the will dies.

FIVE COMMON MISTAKES IN CHOOSING AN EXECUTOR

1. Choosing a contemporary. You want the executor to be able to handle the job when the time comes. Choose someone younger than yourself who is likely to survive you. Or, name a contemporary plus a younger person as co-executor.

2. Choosing the wrong lawyer. If you decide to name an attorney, it should be one whom you know well, not someone you've just met. Nor should you select the lawyer who handled your real estate closing. You need a person who is an expert in trusts and estates. But having said that, never let the lawyer who is preparing your will automatically name himself as executor. This should be your decision and yours alone.

3. Choosing a surviving child.

4. Choosing a family member out of loyalty and love. As much as you want to avoid squabbles and disappointments, your feelings toward family members have no place when it comes to making such a critical decision as this. Unless a family member is *unquestionably qualified*, I urge you to avoid automatically naming a family member as executor. It's important to name an executor who is knowledgeable, is in good health, and can be impartial. And bear in mind that if you have several children, the ones not chosen are likely to be upset.

5. Choosing only one person. If your executor dies before you do and you have not named an alternate in your will, the court will select someone for you. Name an alternate.

Advance Directives

Preparing for incapacity certainly is not a pleasant subject, but we do have to discuss it. It is, unfortunately, a possibility for all of us, in particular because we women are living such long lives.

To address potential incapacity, you need to draw up what are known as advance directives, documents that make certain your wishes concerning physical and financial matters will be carried out if you are unable to do so. Without such directives, your life could fall apart. For example, if no one has the authority to pay your mortgage, you could conceivably lose your house. With no one authorized to pay your bills, your life insurance or medical coverage could be in jeopardy. Advance directives will take care of the bills and other matters.

The three most common advance directives are:

1. Durable power of attorney

2. Health care power of attorney

3. Living will

DURABLE POWER OF ATTORNEY

A power of attorney (POA) is a written document in which you give someone else official authority to act on your behalf. That person is known as your agent or attorney-in-fact. A POA can be a one-time event for something as simple as giving someone authority to sell your car or it can be much broader.

A POA is rarely valid if you become incapacitated. Instead, you need to draw up a durable power of attorney that clearly states you want the power to continue if you become disabled or incapacitated. A durable POA generally remains in effect until you die.

Without such a directive, a family member or friend would have to petition the court to appoint a guardian for you should you become unable to handle your own financial affairs.

Your state may allow you to write your durable power of attorney so it becomes effective only under certain circumstances. This is called a springing POA—that is, the power springs into action only when a specific event or events described in the document occur. The most common, of course, is incapacity.

Among the financial things you might want your attorney-in-fact to be able to take care of are:

- To gain access to your safe deposit box
- To authorize and sign tax returns
- To move you to a state where Medicaid rules are easier to deal with
- To pay your bills
- To deposit your checks
- To make buy-and-sell decisions for stocks, bonds, and mutual funds
- To continue any gifting program you have in place

The person you designate to have this power should be someone you trust completely, someone you know will carry out your wishes and no one else's.

Although it may seem excessive, get at least five or preferably more originals. A growing number of companies and organizations insist upon originals.

You should also check with the financial institutions you use—your bank, brokerage firm, insurance company, mutual funds. Many want the power of attorney drawn on their particular in-house forms. When that's the case, you'll find that the version your attorney drew up on his letterhead may not be acceptable.

Note: You may revoke the power at any time, provided you have capacity. Do so in writing. Destroy all previous copies and notify all third parties in writing.

HEALTH CARE POWER OF ATTORNEY

A durable POA for health care, also called a "health care proxy," is a document appointing someone to act for you when it comes to health decisions. It provides instructions about the extent of medical care and intervention you want to receive in the event of certain problems. Generally, it becomes active only if your physical or mental condition makes it impossible for you to communicate and/or make decisions. It then requires hospitals, nursing homes, doctors, and others to follow your attorney-in-fact's decisions just as though they were your decisions.

However, your attorney-in-fact cannot simply declare you incompetent. A health care POA generally takes effect only when two physicians, including your personal physician, certify that you are not capable of understanding or communicating health decisions.

This type of proxy relieves your family and friends of making very difficult and troubling decisions. Some hospitals even require that you have a power in place before certain types of operations. And in some states, the attorney-in-fact must sign a statement that he or she will not benefit financially should you die. Your attorney can advise you about your state's requirements.

Among the decisions a health care proxy usually covers are:

• To use or withhold life support care

• To use or withhold artificial nutrition and hydration

• To place you in a health facility or to take you out of one

• To deal with Medicare, private insurance companies, and the like

• To make organ donations

A health care proxy does not give authority to your agent regarding financial matters.

> **$TIP: Leave original copies of the durable health care power with your primary physician, your pharmacist, your named agent, and your hospital; keep one additional at home and one in your office.**

Note: A sample health care proxy form is reproduced on page 142.

LIVING WILL

A living will is a written instruction that spells out what treatments you want or do not want in the event that you cannot speak for yourself and you are terminally ill or permanently unconscious.

It is called a living will because it takes effect while you are alive. It is also called a "medical directive."

Note: A sample living will form is reproduced at the end of this chapter.

A DURABLE HEALTH CARE POWER OF ATTORNEY VERSUS A LIVING WILL

It's generally best if you can combine a living will and a durable health care power of attorney in one document, although not all states allow this. Keep in mind that on its own a living will is limited because it usually applies only to terminal illness or a permanent coma. It addresses only life-sustaining medical treatments and not other medical decisions.

A durable health care power of attorney is more comprehensive and more flexible; it is not limited to terminal illness or permanent coma. It authorizes someone to weigh all the facts at a critical time and to speak for you.

About Estate Taxes

The specifics of your estate plan will largely rest on whether or not it is subject to federal estate tax. This tax is incredibly high—in many cases as much as 55%. In addition to estate taxes, the property included in your will may be subject to state death or inheritance taxes as well as state income taxes.

Many women are protected from federal estate taxes by something called the "unified credit." In 2003, it wipes out tax on the first $700,000 worth of otherwise taxable transfers you make through gifts during your lifetime or through your estate after your death. It's called the unified credit because it offsets both the gift tax and the estate tax.

Note: In 2004, the unified credit rises to $850,000; in 2005, $950,000; and in 2006, $1 million. In other words, should you die this year, $700,000 of your assets will be excluded from federal estate tax. If your assets are more than these dollar amounts, your estate will be taxed according to an IRS formula.

If you sense that your estate will be close to these dollar figures within a year or so, speak with your attorney about ways to reduce taxes. (Be sure to include any anticipated inheritance in your calculation.) In the absence of sound estate planning, Uncle Sam will wind up taking a large chunk of your assets. Your lawyer may tell you that one way to sidestep the estate tax due on any dollar amount exceeding these official caps is to leave that "over" amount to charity. Another is to set up a trust.

About Trusts

Trusts come with their own special language and understanding that language will help you in your discussions with your attorney.

- **Trust.** A trust is a legal entity that holds property for the benefit of a specific person, a group of people, or an organization, such as a charity. It can consist of real estate, investments, art, antiques, the right to royalty payments, and so on.

   Trusts can be set up in wills or established while you are still alive.

- **Trustee.** This is the person who takes legal title to the trust property and then administers the property for the benefit of someone else. The trustee can be a reliable friend or relative, a professional, a bank trust department, even the creator of the trust—in the case of a living trust—can be the trustee.

   The trustee must administer the trust according to the trust's provisions.

   You can name a family member (who probably won't charge a fee and generally has a stake in the trust's success) or a professional trustee, such as a bank or attorney, who will

> ## WHY ESTABLISH A TRUST?
>
> Trusts are not just for wealthy people. They can be used by women for many reasons, including:
>
> • To provide for minor children
>
> • To provide for members of your family who are unable to manage their money or other assets
>
> • To provide for the management of your own assets should you become unable to do so yourself
>
> • To avoid probate and transfer your assets immediately and directly to your beneficiaries
>
> • To reduce estate taxes
>
> • To provide for payment of estate taxes
>
> • To maintain privacy; unlike a will, trusts are confidential
>
> • To protect assets from creditors

charge a fee. A professional, however, is unlikely to take sides in family conflicts and has financial and legal expertise that a lay trustee is unlikely to possess. If you have a large estate, I recommend that you name a professional trustee.

• **Benefactor.** This is the person who sets up the trust and provides the funds. The benefactor is also known as the grantor, donor, or settlor.

• **Beneficiary.** The person or persons for whom the trust is created.

• **Remainderman.** The person or persons who will receive the body of the trust when the trust is dissolved. (Charitable trusts may continue forever, but private trusts cannot.)

THE TWO TYPES OF TRUSTS

There are two basic types of trusts: A trust that is created during your lifetime is called a "living" or inter vivas trust. One that comes into being (under the terms of your will) after you die is called a testamentary or "after-death trust."

A Living Trust A living trust, established while you are still alive (hence its name), serves as a partial substitute for a will. You name yourself as the trustee of your own trust and designate someone else as your successor trustee. That person will distribute the assets in the trust if you die and also administer the trust should you be unable to do so due to an illness or accident.

WHY A LIVING TRUST?

The five most common reasons for setting up a living trust for yourself are that:

1. The assets in the trust will not have to go through probate, often a lengthy process and sometimes expensive.

2. The information will remain private; no one will know what you left to whom (wills, on the other hand, are a matter of public record).

3. A trust is less likely to be challenged by relatives or friends who thought you should have done something else with your money.

4. In some states, a living trust will protect the assets against your creditors.

5. If you own real estate in more than one state and it is titled in the trust name, your property will not have to be probated in yet another state.

A living trust can be revocable or irrevocable. Of the two, revocable trusts are more popular because they allow the grantor to make changes to the trust during that person's lifetime.

RENAMING ASSETS

There is one time-consuming task involved: You must rename all of your assets in the trust name, from your savings account to your stock portfolio. This involves contacting your bank, stockbroker, and mutual fund company and setting up new accounts in the trust name, rather than yours. And any real estate you own must be deeded to the trust.

THE TRUSTEE

The trustee you select should have considerable expertise in money management, such as a bank trust department or an investment firm. They will charge an annual fee—probably about 1.5% of the value of the assets under management.

> **$TIP: A living will is rarely a substitute for a will. I strongly urge you to also draw up an old-fashioned will to cover property not taken care of in your living will. And if you have young children, a will is essential as that is the sole document in which you legally name their guardians.**

AN A-TO-Z DIRECTORY OF TRUSTS

Here are thumbnail sketches of the more popular types of trusts. Your attorney may suggest others, but I've included some that apply to couples, should you eventually decide to remarry. Keep in mind that trusts are not for do-it-yourselfers. Consult a knowledgeable attorney. The American College of Trust Estate Counsel (www.actec. org) will help you find a lawyer in your area who specializes in estate planning.

- **Bypass trust.** This allows a married couple to shelter money from estate taxes. The first spouse to die leaves his or her assets in a trust to be used by the surviving spouse for the rest of his or her life. When the second spouse dies, the assets in the trust pass to the children (or other beneficiaries).

- **Charitable trust.** There are several types of charitable trusts that allow you to transfer assets to a trust for the benefit of your favorite charity. They are based on the premise that direct gifts to charity are fully tax deductible. If, for instance, you give your entire estate to a charity, there will be no estate taxes; if you give part away, estate taxes will be reduced.

- **Credit shelter trust.** Should you remarry, you may want to set up this type of trust. It enables you to take advantage of the federal estate tax exemption, which as explained earlier is currently $700,000. In your will, you state that an amount equal to the exemption at the time of your death is to be placed in a credit shelter trust. The rest of your estate goes directly to your spouse. However, he would receive the income and perhaps some of the principal from the trust for his lifetime. When he dies, the assets in the credit shelter trust will be passed on to your children or other heirs, tax free.

- **Life insurance trust.** The IRS requires that insurance be counted as part of your estate. However, by setting up a trust that owns your policy, you can remove insurance from your estate and protect it from federal estate taxes. Proceeds from a life insurance trust, which are administered by a trustee for the beneficiaries, pass directly to the beneficiaries without probate.

- **Living trust.** People who want to avoid probate at all costs like this type of trust. While you're living, you transfer all your assets into a living trust, yet still retain complete control of them. Then, when you die, your assets will be distributed to the people named in the trust without going through probate. *Caution:* The assets, however, are treated as though they had never been put in a trust.

In other words, they are included in your estate tax return and therefore are subject to a tax rate as high as 55%.

- **Medicaid trust.** This trust helps you qualify for federal Medicaid benefits.

- **Qualified personal residence trust.** If you know you want to give your house to your children, you can transfer the title via a qualified personal residence trust. You then have the right to live in the house for a specified number of years. When the trust ends, ownership of the house passes to your children. Even though you've given the house to them, you will not owe gift tax on the entire value of the house; the value is reduced by the value of your right to live in it. You continue to pay the mortgage and taxes while living in the house and, during that time, you can deduct the interest payments and taxes on your 1040 tax return. If you die before the trust ends, the value of the home is included in your estate.

- **Spendthrift trust.** This trust benefits anyone the grantor believes cannot or will not be able to manage their own affairs, such as an extravagant relative.

- **Totten trust.** This is not really a trust at all. It is a type of joint bank account that passes to a named beneficiary immediately upon the owner's death.

NEW YORK HEALTH CARE PROXY

INSTRUCTIONS

PRINT YOUR NAME

(1) I, _____ , hereby appoint:
(name)

_____
(name, home address and telephone number of agent)

PRINT NAME, HOME ADDRESS AND TELEPHONE NUMBER OF YOUR AGENT

_____

as my health care agent to make any and all health care decisions for me, except to the extent that I state otherwise. My agent does know my wishes regarding artificial nutrition and hydration.

This Health Care Proxy shall take effect in the event I become unable to make my own health care decisions.

ADD PERSONAL INSTRUCTIONS (IF ANY)

(2) Optional instructions: I direct my agent to make health care decisions in accord with my wishes and limitations as stated below, or as he or she otherwise knows.

PRINT NAME, HOME ADDRESS AND TELEPHONE NUMBER OF YOUR ALTERNATE AGENT

(3) Name of substitute or fill-in agent if the person I appoint above is unable, unwilling or unavailable to act as my health care agent.

_____
(name, home address and telephone number of alternate agent)

_____

ORGAN DONATION (OPTIONAL)

(4) Donation of Organs at Death: Upon my death:

[   ] I **do not** wish to donate my organs, tissues or parts.
[   ] I **do** wish to be an organ donor and upon my death I wish to donate:

ORGAN DONATION (OPTIONAL) CONTINUED

[   ] (a) Any needed organs, tissues, or parts;

OR

[   ] (b) The following organs, tissues, or parts

_____

_____

[   ] (c) My gift is for the following purposes:
(put a line through any of the following you do
not want)
(i) Transplant   (iii) Research
(ii) Therapy   (iv) Education

ENTER A DURATION OR A CONDITION (IF ANY)

(5) Unless I revoke it, this proxy shall remain in effect indefinitely, or until the date or condition I have stated below. This proxy shall expire (specific date or conditions, if desired): _____

_____

SIGN AND DATE THE DOCUMENT AND PRINT YOUR ADDRESS

(6) Signature _____ Date _____
Address _____

Statement by Witnesses (must be 18 or older)

WITNESSING PROCEDURE

I declare that the person who signed this document appeared to execute the proxy willingly and free from duress. He or she signed (or asked another to sign for him or her) this document in my presence. I am not the person appointed as proxy by this document.

YOUR WITNESSES MUST SIGN AND PRINT THEIR ADDRESSES

Witness 1 _____
Address _____

Witness 2 _____
Address _____

Courtesy of Partnership for Caring, Inc.   *12/00*
1620 Eye Street, NW., Suite 202, Washington, DC 20006   800-989-9455

NEW YORK LIVING WILL

This Living Will has been prepared to conform to the law in the State of New York, as set forth in the case In re Westchester County Medical Center, 72 N.Y.2d 517 (1988). In that case the Court established the need for "clear and convincing" evidence of a patient's wishes and stated that the "ideal situation is one in which the patient's wishes were expressed in some form of writing, perhaps a 'living will.'"

PRINT YOUR NAME

I, _____, being of sound mind, make this statement as a directive to be followed if I become permanently unable to participate in decisions regarding my medical care. These instructions reflect my firm and settled commitment to decline medical treatment under the circumstances indicated below:

I direct my attending physician to withhold or withdraw treatment that merely prolongs my dying, if I should be in an **incurable or irreversible mental or physical condition with no reasonable expectation of recovery,** including but not limited to: (a) **a terminal condition;** (b) **a permanently unconscious condition;** or (c) **a minimally conscious condition in which I am permanently unable to make decisions or express my wishes.**

I direct that my treatment be limited to measures to keep me comfortable and to relieve pain, including any pain that might occur by withholding or withdrawing treatment.

CROSS OUT ANY STATEMENTS THAT DO NOT REFLECT YOUR WISHES

While I understand that I am not legally required to be specific about future treatments **if I am in the condition(s) described above I feel especially strongly about the following forms of treatment:**

I do not want cardiac resuscitation.
I do not want mechanical respiration.
I do not want artificial nutrition and hydration.
I do not want antibiotics.

However, I **do want** maximum pain relief, even if it may hasten my death.

Other directions:

These directions express my legal right to refuse treatment, under the law of New York. I intend my instructions to be carried out, unless I have rescinded them in a new writing or by clearly indicating that I have changed my mind.

Signed _____ Date _____
Address _____

I declare that the person who signed this document appeared to execute the living will willingly and free from duress. He or she signed (or asked another to sign for him or her) this document in my presence.

Witness 1 _____
Address _____

Witness 2 _____
Address _____

For More Help

Partnership for Caring (800-989-WILL or www.choices.org) has free examples of a living will and a medical power of attorney.

National Network of Estate Planning Attorneys (800-638-8681 or www.netplanning.com/consumer) is sponsored by a for-profit group of estate planning attorneys. They will help you find an attorney in your area and provide consumer information.

Plan Your Estate is published by The Vanguard Group (800-871-3879 or www.vanguard.com/?PlainTalk). It covers the steps to take before seeing a professional estate planner, with a focus on trusts and taxes.

Chapter Twelve

IMPORTANT PAPERS

*I'm proud to be paying taxes in the United States. The only
thing is . . . I could be just as proud for half the money.*
— ARTHUR GODFREY

If your husband did more than you in the area of doing your tax return and bill paying, you may be wondering what documents you need to keep, where you need to keep them, and for how long.

What to Keep and for How Long

Sometimes it pays to be a pack rat because tossing out papers you need not only could cost you money but also certainly will eat up hours of time as you try to replace the lost information. Although I'm not by nature overly conservative, I am in this area because I know how demanding and unforgiving the IRS can be. You should be extra cautious too.

TAX RETURNS

The IRS has three years from your filing date to audit your return if it suspects a "good faith" error. The three-year deadline also applies if *you* discover a mistake in your return and decide to file an amended return to claim a refund.

The IRS has six years to challenge your return if it thinks you underreported your gross income by 25% or more.

It can come after you forever if you failed to file a return or filed a fraudulent one. State tax rules vary, so check with a local accountant.

CANCELED CHECKS

Keep those relating to your taxes for six years. These include mortgage payments, business expenses, charitable contributions, child care, medical expenses, professional dues, retirement plan contributions, and, if you're the one paying, alimony.

BROKERAGE STATEMENTS

Keep records of stock and bond purchases as well as the actual certificates until you sell them. You need to prove whether you have a capital gain or loss when you file your tax return.

> $TIP: If you are keeping stock and bond certificates in your safe deposit box, rather than leaving them *in street name,* photocopy each one and store copies in a location separate from the originals.

MUTUAL FUNDS

As with stocks and bonds, you must pay taxes on any price appreciation when you sell fund shares. Therefore, when you buy shares of a mutual fund, keep the confirmation slip indicating the number of shares you bought and what you paid for them.

> $TIP: If you decide to sell only some of your shares, your records will help you decide which ones to unload. The IRS assumes that you are selling the first shares you purchased, unless you specify to the

contrary. This is called "first in, first out" (FIFO) and can be unnecessarily costly if you have regularly purchased in a fund that has continually increased in value.

REAL ESTATE INFORMATION

If you own a house, condo, or co-op, keep all records showing the purchase price and the cost of permanent improvements (new roof, electrical wiring, an addition, installation of air-conditioning, major remodeling). Also keep records of expenses related to buying and/or selling property—such as legal fees, property searches, advertising, and appraisals—for six years after you sell your property.

PAYCHECK STUBS

Keep these until you receive your annual W-2 Form from your employer. Make certain the dollar amounts agree. If it doesn't, ask for a corrected form, known as a W-2C. You should also save your final paycheck of the year; it records deductions for pension contributions, deductible medical insurance premiums, charitable contributions, and union dues, all of which have tax implications.

CREDIT CARD STUFF

Keep original receipts until you receive your monthly statement. Then you can toss them if there are no errors. Keep monthly statements for six years if anything is tax related, including business expenses. If your credit card gives you buyer protection or has an extended warranty plan, keep these perks until they expire.

If you have charged big ticket items, such as jewelry, antiques, rugs, collectibles, furniture, computers and printers, appliances, motorcycles, and so on, the individual bill or the specific credit card statement for that charge should be kept to use as proof of their value in case they are stolen, lost, or damaged.

MATURED BANK CDS

Save until January of the year after they've matured. That's when you get a form from the bank indicating how much interest you have earned.

RETIREMENT PLAN DATA

Keep quarterly 401(k) or 403(b) and pension plan statements until the end of the year. If everything matches, keep only the annual statements. I recommend that you keep those until you retire or close your account.

> **$TIP:** If you made a nondeductible contribution to an IRA, keep records forever because when you start to withdraw money, you will need to prove that you've already paid taxes on these contributions. (You need to file Form #8606 if you made a nondeductible IRA contribution.)

For More Help

Recordkeeping for Individuals, IRS Publication #552 (www.irs.gov)

Where to Keep Important Documents

Not all important papers belong in your safe deposit box, not all in your at-home files. Here's where to keep what.

- **Your will.** Leave the original with the attorney who drafted it. (Make sure he/she has a fireproof vault or a bank vault.) Keep one copy at home and one in your safe deposit box. Write your attorney's address and phone number on the copies. *Caution:* Do not put your original (or the only copy) in your safe deposit box; in many states, you cannot get immediate access when the owner of the box dies nor are most banks open on weekends and holidays.

A PERSONAL DIRECTORY

To make it easier for someone else to manage your financial affairs if you are traveling or become ill—and to save yourself time—make a list of the following and where they are located. When appropriate, note the account number, addresses, and phone number.

☐ Accountant

☐ Attorney

☐ Automobile loan

☐ Bank accounts

☐ Birth, marriage, and divorce certificates

☐ Brokerage accounts

☐ Credit card loans

☐ Drivers license

☐ Employer

☐ Financial adviser

☐ Hidden cash, jewelry, silver

☐ Insurance policies

☐ Insurance agent

☐ Medicare, Medigap, or health insurance card

☐ Minister, priest, rabbi

☐ Mortgage papers

☐ Mutual fund accounts

☐ Passport

☐ Personal loans

☐ Physicians

☐ Retirement accounts

☐ Social Security card

☐ Stockbroker

☐ Student loans

- **Your letter of instruction.** A letter telling your family what your wishes are concerning your funeral arrangements and other matters should be in your personal file at home. You should also tell at least one member of your family where it is located.

- **Durable power of attorney.** A signed copy should be given to the person named to act on your behalf in financial matters should you not be able to handle them and to your attorney. Keep one copy at home.

- **Health care proxy and living will.** Give signed copies of both to the person(s) named to speak on your behalf and to each doctor named in the document.

- **Living trusts.** Leave the original with your attorney. Keep a copy at home and give a copy to your co-trustees and any backup trustees.

- **Birth, marriage, and divorce certificates.** Keep the originals in your safe deposit box and copies at home and with your attorney.

- **Insurance policies.** Keep the original in your safe deposit box and a copy at home.

- **Your husband's death certificate.** You and your attorney should each have certified copies. Put one in your safe deposit box and keep several at home.

- **Other papers.** Your attorney, your accountant, and/or a member of your family should know where you've filed your old tax returns, insurance policies, leases, mortgage documents, and bank account records.

> **$TIP:** If you've given someone power of attorney, be sure that person is aware of key papers and your blank checks.

Bottom Line

Ray Kroc, founder of McDonald's gave the best advice about being organized: "We work on the KISS system. KISS is the acronym for 'Keep It Simple, Stupid.'" Now that you have finished this section, I hope that you have adopted a simple, streamlined system—and no one will be calling you stupid.

Section Five

Your New Life

Chapter Thirteen

YOUR HOUSE: STAYING PUT

A man's home is his castle.
—SIR EDWARD COKE
(AND A WOMAN'S TOO . . .)

The one topic you'll get lots of advice about from well-meaning friends is where you live. Older children may want you to move in with them or somewhere nearby. If you are a very young widow, your parents or in-laws may suggest you join them. Others will tell you to begin life anew in the city or the country. Some will suggest moving to a less expensive place.

One of the biggest mistakes that a widow can make is selling her house or giving up her apartment within months of her husband's death. Understandably she may do so because it is so painful to stay in the same place where she lived with her spouse. But you should make every effort to resist the rush to move. You need time to sort out things, to adjust to living on your own, to determine what is best for you, both financially and emotionally.

So please read through this chapter and Chapter 14 on moving, no matter what your shelter needs and concerns, and then make your decision, free from pressure.

Going from Joint to Single Ownership

I want to begin by giving you permission to temporarily keep your utility and telephone bills in your husband's name or joint names—if that's how it's been. This is not a long-term solution but, for a while, it will help keep at bay those dreadful people who prey on widows.

Many couples hold their house in joint tenancy (see Chapter 2). The major advantage to doing so is that when one joint owner dies, the remaining owner automatically inherits the deceased's portion of the property without having to go through the probate process. If, however, you owned your house with tenancy in common, then you both owned equal shares. Upon your husband's death, his share went to whomever he named in his will or other estate-planning document—probably you. If he died without a will, his share passed under the laws of your state and, again, most likely his came to you.

If the house is now yours, have your attorney change the title to reflect your sole ownership.

Renting for Income

A major factor in deciding whether to remain in your house or move is financial. In Chapter 6 you drew up your cash flow statement. If you know you have sufficient income to comfortably stay put, then you can skip this section. If you are having trouble making ends meet, your house can be a source of income in a number of ways: by renting, _refinancing_, or getting a _home equity loan_ or a _second mortgage_. If you are a senior citizen, you can take out a _reverse mortgage_. Let's start with the easiest: renting.

Renting out unused space may be an excellent temporary solution. For some widows, especially those living alone, it often turns into a very comfortable long-term solution.

There are a number of possibilities. You can rent a bedroom and bath to someone on a full-time basis—that is, the renter signs a lease for six months or a year. Or, you can rent to someone who needs housing on a temporary basis, such as a teacher or a professional who has been transferred into your area and is looking for a house to buy. I have a friend who rents space in someone's house so she can write her novels in peace and quiet. Their arrangement allows the writer to use a study/bedroom, bath, and kitchen four mornings a week. Homeowners can also rent out a garage or storage space. If you have a very spacious house, you might do what Florence Griswold (1850–1937) did in Old Lyme, Connecticut. She housed talented painters and sculptors, turning her mansion and carriage houses into an art colony with studios. Today it is the Florence Griswold Museum.

However, proceed with caution. Interview prospective renters with someone else present—your attorney or one of your adult children. Check at least three personal and three business references. Have a clearly written lease in which you require one or two month's security deposit. You may want to add certain items to the lease regarding noise level (radio, TV, CD player), guests, pets, children, alcohol, and smoking. Stipulate whether or not the renter may use your kitchen. And, check your homeowner's insurance policy to make certain you are adequately covered in case your renter has an accident, is injured, or for some reason decides to sue you.

Refinancing Your Mortgage

If you decide to stay where you are for at least several years, you might want to consider refinancing—that is, paying off your old mortgage for a new one with more favorable terms. But even if interest rates are low, don't refinance just to refinance. It's not a free process. It involves paying a number of fees.

Refinancing can reduce your monthly payments, giving you money to invest, to save, or to pay off debt. It can even shorten the number of years on your loan and thus save thousands of dollars in interest payments.

Caution: If your current mortgage contains a prepayment penalty, you may find it difficult to make refinancing worthwhile, as the penalty could offset any savings you would gain by refinancing.

Whether or not refinancing makes sense depends on how long you plan to stay in your house, how much you have left on your current mortgage, the terms of a new mortgage, and closing costs. In general, the longer you plan to live in your home after you refinance, the better because it gives you time to recoup financing costs and then to begin to save money.

The best way to determine whether or not to refinance is to run the numbers through an online calculator (two of the best calculators are Quicken's Refinance Calculator [www.quicken.com] and The Motley Fool's [www.fool.com]), or to ask your accountant to help you. Mortgage brokers are also experts in this field. But before doing so, you need to gather these facts for inputting:

Your Current Mortgage:

- The outstanding balance or dollar amount left on your current mortgage

- The remaining number of years on your current mortgage

- The current interest rate on your loan

Your Proposed Loan:

- The term (or number of years) of the new loan

- The interest rate you want to pay on the new loan (*Note:* Most calculators will give you the national average rate.)

- The estimated closing costs (The standard closing expenses are the application fee, a credit check, your attorney's fees, the lender's attorney's fees, the title search, the title insurance, the appraisal fee, inspections, preparation of documents, and points. [Each point is 1% of the amount of the loan.] Some states also charge "mortgage taxes." Assume that total closing costs will add up to as much as 7% of the purchase cost.)

- How many years you plan to live in your home

Note: The people who put the calculators together realize you may not know what your closing costs will be or how long you'll stay in your house, so you can simply select the national average that is provided. However, the rule of thumb is expect to pay 3% to 6% of the outstanding principal in refinancing costs. So if your outstanding <u>principal</u> is $60,000, expect refinancing costs to run between $1,800 and $3,600. Add to that any prepayment penalty—if you have one.

> **$TIP: Don't use Fannie Mae's (www.finaniemae. com) calculator; it's too simplistic to be truly useful. However, the Glossary of Real Estate and Mortgage Terms on this site is the best around.**

Your current lender may offer the best deal because they don't want to lose your business. Ask your lender to figure out what your new payments would be with a lower rate. And, sometimes the company carrying the present title insurance policy will reissue your policy at a reduced reissue rate. This could save you up to 70% versus drawing up a new policy.

Once you've received a quote from your current lender, don't stop there. It's essential that you shop for rates; they vary from lender to lender and from city to city, and you may find a better deal somewhere else. I recommend that you check with at least four lenders. Two websites that make rate shopping easy are HSH Associates (www. hsh.com) and Bank Rate Monitor (www.bankrate.com). Both provide continually updated rates from around the country. Neither is in the business of selling mortgages. Then, check the lenders listed in the box below.

Finally, don't overlook your local newspaper. Websites may not include all the lenders in your area, especially if you live in a small

THREE PLACES TO FIND MORTGAGES ONLINE

- Countrywide:
  www.countrywide.com

- Lending Tree:
  www.lendingtree.com

- Quicken:
  www.quickenmortgage.com

town or a rural section of the country. Your paper may, in fact, turn up the best deal.

Once you've found the right refinancing package, make certain it does not come with a prepayment penalty or any other restrictions that prevent your ability to refinance again. You never know when rates may fall even lower.

For More Help

Fannie Mae (800-732-6643 or www.homepath.com) has free brochures on buying a home, getting a mortgage, and refinancing.

Mortgage Bankers Association (202-557-2700 or www.mbaa.org) has an excellent glossary of terms and tips on refinancing as well as a brochure titled *Refinancing, Does It Make Cents For You?*

Home Equity Loans

Another way you can use your house as a source of cash is with a home equity loan. If you're thinking about adding on a deck or fixing up the kitchen or if tuition payments are just around the corner, one way to pay for these and other major expenses is with a home equity loan. But don't rush to take your lender to lunch. These loans, like most things financial, come with the good and the bad. Before signing on the dotted line, here's what you need to know.

Right up front, I want to warn you that although home equity loans are an easy and tax-deductible way to use your house as a source of cash, they are not a good idea unless you are 100% confident that you can make the payments. You are putting your biggest asset—your house—on the line and, if you don't pay back the loan, the bank can _foreclose_. Foreclosure means not having a place to sleep. And no SUV or Sub-Zero is worth that price.

On the other hand, if you have a secure job and you stick to the budget we worked out in Chapter 6, these loans can be a smart way to purchase big-ticket items or pay off high-interest-rate credit card debt. They should never, ever be used to pay for your vacation, finance a junket to Las Vegas, or spruce up your wardrobe.

They also come with a very nice tax advantage: you can deduct up to $100,000 worth of interest payments on your federal tax return, so it often makes sense to move loans where the interest is not tax deductible—on your BMW, Harley, Visa, or MasterCard, for example—over to a tax-deductible home equity loan.

Home equity loans come in two types: term loans and line of credit loans. Bankers often refer to them as second mortgages because, just like your first mortgage, your house secures the loan.

THE HOME EQUITY TERM OR CLOSED-END LOAN

This is a one-time lump-sum loan that you pay off over for a fixed period of time at a fixed rate of interest. Your payments will be the same, month after month. Once you've received the lump sum, you are not entitled to additional funds. This loan, which is very similar to a first mortgage, enables you to know in advance exactly what your payments will be.

THE HOME EQUITY LINE OF CREDIT

Lenders refer to this open-end loan, which is much like a credit card loan, by its initials, HELOC. The lender decides in advance how much you can borrow for a given period of time. During that time frame, you can tap into your preapproved line of credit when needed. That means, you only pay for the money that you actually borrow.

As you pay back your loan, your credit can be used again. If, for example, you have a $20,000 line of credit and you borrow $10,000. Several months later, you pay back $5,000. You now have $15,000 immediately available.

The HELOC has a variable rate of interest that fluctuates over the span of the loan. That means the loan has an unpredictability about it because the monthly payments vary based on the interest rate and how much credit you have used.

HELOCs can be accessed at any time by check, a special type credit or ATM card, or, in some cases, by phone.

You must have paid back the loan in full when the stated time period is up. At that point, your lender may or may not allow you to renew your line of credit.

WHICH TYPE SHOULD YOU PICK?

The answer is subject to many generalizations and so, like all generalizations, there are exceptions. Add your own common sense to my suggestions.

Scenario #1: Your Daughter's Wedding or a New Bathroom Your daughter is getting married in six months and you plan to help with the expenses. You know in advance that you will need about $6,000.

You've decided, after years of sharing the same tub and sink with your kids, that it's time you had your own bathroom. Your contractor informs you this will cost approximately $4,250.

These two examples call for a fixed-rate term home equity loan because you know how much you will need, when you will need it, and that you must pay both the caterer and the contractor within 30 days, maybe 60 if you're lucky.

A fixed-rate term, especially when rates are low, is also the loan of choice for paying off high-interest-rate credit card debt.

Therefore, the home equity term or closed-end loan is best if you are borrowing to fund a one-time project or purchase.

Scenario #2: Your Son's Tuition or a New Wing on the House Tuition at most schools comes due twice a year, for four years. Building a new wing or other major renovation may be a one- to two-year program, with payments to various contractors spread out over time. A HELOC works well in both these cases because you can tap into it over a longer time period, but only as payments are required.

Therefore, a HELOC is best if you have an ongoing project or serial payments to make.

THE GOOD, THE BAD, AND HOW MUCH

First, the bad . . .

Neither type of home equity loan is a good idea for widows who lack substantial savings and disposable income. Unless you are earning a very high salary and your job is very secure, taking on yet another loan makes it very easy to fall behind on payments and wind up over your head in debt.

> **$TIP: The total of all your debt payments—mortgages, credit cards, auto loans, student loans, and so on should not be more than 36% of your gross monthly income.**

Nor are home equity loans recommended for most older people. Once you are living on a fixed income, you don't want to have even one set of mortgage payments, let alone two. And, should you decide upon retirement to downsize, you want to have plenty of cash left over after selling your house in order to buy a smaller one, mortgage-free.

Another word of caution: with the HELOC, when interest rates rise, your payments will also rise. This can spell trouble if your salary or income remains the same.

And now the good . . .

If you can easily cover both an original mortgage (if you have one) and a second one and if the need for the loan is a sensible one, then this is a smart time to access the equity in your house. This is especially smart when rates are low. But like everything else economic, they are cyclical. Eventually they will rise. You'd be wise to lock in your loan when the time is right.

And lastly, how much . . .

Most lenders cap the credit line at 80% of the appraised value of your home minus the balance of your mortgage. (Your other debts, credit history, and income will also be considered.) Let's say you still owe $25,000 on your mortgage and your house is appraised at

COMPARING LOAN RATES (AS OF DECEMBER 2002)	
Credit Card Loan	12%–16%
Conventional Mortgage	5.5%
Home Equity Term Loan	7.0%
Home Equity Line of Credit	5.0%

$125,000. Your equity or "loan-to-value" then is $100,000. A standard home equity loan would be 80% of that amount or $80,000.

Even though some lenders will lend you more—up to 125%—don't go down that path. It may be very difficult to make payments, especially if you lose your job or face serious medical problems.

Although a home equity line of credit is cheaper than a credit card loan and the interest is tax deductible, you should not take out this kind of loan unless you are self-disciplined and know you can repay it on time. Not only does the loan reduce the equity in your home, it makes it terribly easy to spend and spend and spend.

For More Help

Microsoft (www.msn.com; click on "House & Home") has three useful calculators in the "Financing" section: Home Equity Credit Limits, Estimated Home Equity Payments, and Figure Tax Savings.

Interest.com (www.interest.com) has calculators that help you determine which type of loan is better as well as how much interest you will pay.

When Your Home Is on the Line: What You Should Know about Home Equity Lines of Credit addresses common questions and provides terms, tips, a checklist, and how to find the plan that meets your needs and protects your interest. (Download for free at www.pueblo.gsa.gov or for a 50 cents mailing charge, call 888-878-3256.)

Reverse Mortgages

A reverse mortgage allows people 62 and older to borrow against the equity in their homes and at the same time continue to live in them. It's a way to keep a roof over your head while supplementing your income. You receive money in one of three ways: a lump sum, on a regular monthly basis, or as a line of credit that can be tapped when needed. The dollar amount depends on the age and value of your house, its location, and the cost of the loan itself.

Unlike traditional mortgages and home equity loans, there's no repayment until you are no longer living in your home. In other words, the mortgage is repaid when the homeowner moves (perhaps to a retirement community, in with children, or to a nursing home) or dies. Then, the homeowner's estate pays off the debt, usually by selling the property.

Caution: Because you are not making monthly payments on your loan, the *amount you owe grows over time,* while the amount of cash you or your estate will have left after selling the house and paying off the loan declines. However, you can never owe more than the value of your home at the time the loan is repaid.

To qualify, in addition to being at least 62, you must own and occupy the house as a principal residence. And there must be no mortgage or very little mortgage left, like one to three payments.

Getting a reverse mortgage doesn't mean you can give up mowing the lawn. Borrowers must continue to pay property taxes and insurance as well as make repairs to maintain the value of the house.

Fees and expenses can be substantial. Most participating banks charge at least 1% over the current rate for conventional mortgages. Add to that a 2% origination fee, a 1% insurance fee, an appraisal, and a credit report. (The 1% insurance fee protects the bank against the risk that you will live so long that your loan will be greater than your equity. But the reverse mortgage is generally structured to avoid this happening.)

$TIP: You may be able to set up an "all in the family" reverse mortgage if you have relatives who are financially able to give you monthly income in exchange for ownership of your house when you die.

Below are five protective steps you should take if you are considering a reverse mortgage:

1. Learn. This is a complicated program. Don't be embarrassed if you don't understand all the details. And don't make a decision in a hurry, under pressure.

2. Take someone with you. Ask your lawyer, your accountant, or a family member to accompany you when you meet with the lender.

3. Comparison shop. Call several lenders in your area.

4. Skip it. This type of loan is too expensive for small amounts of money. And skip it entirely if you know you will be staying in your house less than five years.

5. Consider selling. You might be better off if you simply sell your house and buy a less expensive one. As pointed out above, if you qualify, you can exclude up to $250,000 from capital gains tax. (See "Selling versus Renting" on page 175.)

For More Help

American Association of Retired Persons (800-424-3410 or www.aarp.org/revmort) publishes *Home Made Money: A Consumer Guide To Reverse Mortgages*.

Fannie Mae (800-732-6643 or www.fanniemae.com) will send you a list of reverse mortgage lenders in your area along with free literature explaining how these mortgages work and what to watch out for.

HUD (800-424-3410) offers free literature on reverse mortgages plus a list of lenders.

The National Reverse Mortgage Lenders Association (202-939-1760 or www.reversemortgage.org) provides lists of lenders and consumer literature on the process.

Redecorating and Remodeling

When George S. Kaufman first saw his partner Moss Hart's remodeled estate, he said, "That's what God would have done if he had the money."

You don't need to go overboard à la Moss Hart and turn your house into a castle, but many widows really do find it easier to continue living in the house they shared with their husband if they make a few simple changes. Wallpapering, a fresh coat of pain, and planting tulip bulbs can make you feel brighter and more oriented toward the future. And, the process of planning such projects will give you a focus and keep you busy. Of course, decorating with a talented friend or a professional will make it all the more social.

REMODELING

You may want to undertake something more major than new drapes or painting the window boxes, particularly if your house has become dated or if you need additional room for guests or an office. Certain remodeling jobs actually increase the value of property and pay off when and if you sell. At the top of this list are bathrooms and kitchens. According to *Remodeling* magazine, the national average of putting in a new bathroom is $14,216. You can expect to recoup 82% of that amount. A major kitchen remodeling runs about $38,700, and you'll get back 81% of the cost. Adding on a deck averages $5,685 of which you'll recoup 76%. Other projects that pay off include adding a family room, turning attic space into a bedroom, and redoing the master bedroom.

If you decide to overhaul your kitchen or fix up the potting shed, keep in mind that your house or apartment will actually become the work site. You will be living with the project from beginning to end.

That means making changes in your daily routine and being surrounded by workmen and equipment. It can be a messy business. On the other hand, you may delight in having people around and in watching the progress of your remodeling job.

Unless you're handy with a hammer and saw, you'll have to hire a pro. A key to the success of remodeling is getting the right contractor or handyman. Begin by checking with neighbors and friends; ask for names of those they liked and those in whom they were disappointed.

Then get all remodeling estimates in writing, with at least two people bidding on the project. Pay your contractor or handyman as you go along, with the final payment dependent upon the satisfactory completion of the job. This installment-type schedule should be included in your written contract to avoid any confusion.

Keep accurate records of all home improvements. The money spent to improve a house (as opposed to money spent on upkeep and maintenance) reduces the capital gains tax when the house is sold.

The following expenses qualify as capital improvements:

- ☐ A new room, porch, deck, or garage
- ☐ All new windows
- ☐ Central air-conditioning
- ☐ Central vacuuming system
- ☐ Drapery rods
- ☐ Built-in appliances in the kitchen
- ☐ Insulation
- ☐ New boiler
- ☐ New plumbing
- ☐ New roof
- ☐ New wiring
- ☐ Pavement on the driveway
- ☐ A fence
- ☐ A septic system
- ☐ A soft water system
- ☐ A sprinkler system
- ☐ A swimming pool
- ☐ Venetian blinds

Repairs fall more into the decorating category as far as the IRS is concerned. Repairs include such things as:

- ☐ Fixing a leak
- ☐ Minor plastering
- ☐ Painting
- ☐ Replacing a broken window
- ☐ Replacing broken or cracked tiles
- ☐ Making small gutter repairs
- ☐ Wallpapering

However, the IRS never makes things simple. If you are doing a total renovation of a room, then painting and wallpapering could conceivably be a capital improvement.

BRING IN THE EXPERTS

No matter what redecorating or renovation you plan, it generally pays in the long run to call in expert advice.

- **Architects.** Licensed by the state, architects are qualified to develop construction plans that meet local building and fire codes. Get in touch with the American Institute of Architects (800-242-3837 or www.aiaaccess.com) for a local chapter near you.

- **Contractors.** Licensed by the state, contractors are often general builders and oversee large projects. But many states require that specialists be licensed in their area of expertise. California, for example, has over 40 different types of licenses including roof repair, plumbing, and electrical repair. Any job that costs $500 or more for material and labor must have a licensed contractor. Check with your state and always ask to see a contractor's number and one other form of ID.

- **Handymen.** Members of the Handyman Connection (www.handymanconnection.com), started in 1990, are bonded and insured. The company, with franchises in the 48 contiguous states, specializes in completing small- to medium-size home repairs and remodeling jobs. All work is done by retired craftsmen who must have a minimum of ten years experience in their trade. They pride themselves on the fact that no job is too small. Among the services offered: carpentry, plumbing, dry wall, ceramic tile, painting, and plastering. All work is guaranteed for one year.

- **Interior designers.** These professionals will transform an existing space into something new. Those who are members of the American Society of Interior Designers (ASID) (800-775-2743 or www.interiors.org) or certified by the National Council for Interior Design (NCIDQ) are accredited and can advise clients on all elements of design. (In a handful of states, interior designers must take a professional exam, be licensed, and fulfill continuing education requirements.)

- **Interior decorators.** These consultants cannot make structural changes, although they can make verbal recommendations. They will help you with color schemes, fabrics, furnishings, paintings, window treatments, rugs, and room arrangements. They can also take you to individual designer showrooms to select fabrics, wallpapers, lighting fixtures, rugs, and furniture. The prices on items charged will be at a discount from retail; however, the decorator's fee in some cases may almost make up the difference. To find a decorator in your area, check with the Interior Arrangement & Design Association (www.interiorarrangement. org) or the Certified Interior Decorators Organization (www. certifiedinteriordecorators.org).

- **Remodelers.** The Remodelers Council, a division of the National Association of Home Builders (800-223-2665 or www. nahb.org), sponsors a professional program called Certified Graduate Remodeler (CGR). If at all possible, protect yourself by working with a remodeler who has this designation. It means he or she has completed the program's educational requirements and has met its prescribed standards of business experience and practices.

- **Repairmen.** All members of Service Magic (www.servicemagic. com) who pay a one-time $99 activation fee are prescreened. That means they must have clean legal and credit history, be licensed and insured, plus have a minimum of three satisfied customer ratings. After completing a survey about your needs, Service Magic will email you the names of four prescreened professionals in your area.

> **$TIP:** Service Magic's "Project Estimator" will help you determine the approximate cost of a project (painting, wallpapering, building additions, roofing, cleaning, landscaping, installing ramps, putting up fences, and more). The estimator is zip code sensitive so you can budget more accurately.

PAYING THE BILL

If you have enough cash on hand, this of course is the least expensive way to pay for a remodeling project. You could also arrange for a home equity loan (described earlier in this chapter) or a home improvement loan (described later in this chapter). Interest payments on both are tax deductible.

An excellent source for home improvement loans is the Federal Housing Administration (FHA). These fixed-rate loans that the FHA insures against risk of default come with caps—up to $25,000 for a single family home and up to $60,000 for a multi-family structure. For information and a list of approved lenders in your area, go to www.hud.gov and click on "Home Improvement."

Once you've decided how much you can afford to spend on redecorating or remodeling, make sure you stick to your budget. The National Association of Home Builders recommends that you:

- Plan on spending only 80% of what you can afford. Put the other 20% in a savings account and use it to cover changes and unanticipated problems.

- Think about all the details. Anything not included in the original contract will cost extra. This could mean tacking on hundreds of dollars to the original price.

- Stick with the project planned. Don't go overboard and overhaul your entire house.

For More Help

Remodeling magazine (www.remodeling.hw.net) has an annual cost versus value report. You can search by project or by geographical region.

The National Association of Home Builders (800-223-2665 or www.nahb.org) has a number of free, helpful publications including *How to Live with Your Remodeling Project, Protecting Yourself from Contractor Fraud,* and *Understanding Your Remodeling Contract.*

Hometime (www.hometime.com) is an entertaining yet immensely helpful home improvement show on public television. The website will tell you when the show airs in your area.

The Do It Yourself Network (www.diynet.com) is available on cable TV in most parts of the country. This channel covers just about everything, from cleaning your house to landscaping, decorating, and remodeling.

Family Handyman magazine (800-285-4961 or www.familyhandyman.com) is a Reader's Digest publication with a wealth of practical information, ranging from how to fix your leaking roof and put up a chair rail to which tools are must-haves.

This Old House magazine (www.thisoldhousemagazine.com) has tips on such diverse topics as replacing a kitchen sink, tiling a floor, and installing a lockset. The section on projects you can do in a weekend is especially helpful.

Home Tips (www.hometips.com) is an excellent source if you're making small repairs such as replacing a dimmer switch, fixing a window pain, or stopping a leaky faucet. It has good material on cutting heating and air-conditioning costs.

411 Home Repair (www.homerepair.com) provides detailed instructions on such topics as replacing tiles, hanging wallpaper, or landscaping your backyard.

Decorator's Secrets (www.decoratorsecrets.com) offers many useful services, including sample color guides.

Use What You Have Decorating (www.redecorate.com) offers very reasonable fee-based consultation with members of the Interior Refiner's Network.

Department of Housing & Urban Development (www.hud.gov) has a free publication, *Protect Yourself: Deceptive Home Improvement Contractors,* which includes a section on what to do if you're "taken."

Chapter Fourteen

YOUR HOUSE: MOVING

In my father's house, there are many mansions.

—John 14:2

In the previous chapter, I strongly urged you not to move within the first months after your husband's death. However, if enough time has passed for you to be able to think a little more clearly and not be pressured by others, moving might be just the right step. There are many "mansions" in our lives and, for you, it may be a less expensive one in your current neighborhood, a place near your adult children, or a rental in your old hometown. A new job may lure you to another part of the country. If you haven't got it all plotted out, read on.

To Move or Not to Move: Testing the Waters

If you are seriously considering the idea of moving to a smaller place or to live in a <u>co-op</u> or <u>condominium</u> where someone else will mow the lawn, rake the leaves, and shovel the snow, I recommend that you test the water first. Rent an apartment or townhouse for a month or a season. Try living with your kids for the summer. (Why not rent out your own house for extra income while you're testing the water?) What may have seemed like an ideal place when you were on a holiday or short visit may not be quite so ideal once you spend an extended period of time there. You may love your grandchildren and

SELLING VERSUS RENTING

If you are thinking of selling your house and moving to a rental, first review the benefits of ownership and then discuss the tax-related ones with your accountant. Keep in mind that 8% to 10% of the value of your home goes into selling; including moving expenses, closing costs, and brokers' fees.

When you own . . .

- You build up equity. Equity is the current market value of the house minus all mortgages.

- You have something to borrow against. Should you need to, you can borrow against the equity value—even before you've paid off your mortgage. And for older women, a reverse mortgage (explained later in this chapter) can be a welcome source of cash.

- You can take tax deductions. The interest you pay on the mortgage as well as your real estate taxes are deductible.

- You have property you can rent. This gives you the flexibility of traveling, going back to school, or taking on a work assignment out of town.

- You can pocket up to $250,000 in profits. Under the new tax regulations, this amount is free from capital gains taxes when you sell a primary residence. You must have lived in the house for at least two of the last five years. You can actually do this as often as every two years.

- You can keep your house when you go on Medicaid. In most states, your primary residence is exempt when trying to qualify for Medicaid benefits. (See Chapter 8 for more details.)

Renting versus Buying

One of the best ways to determine how much you'll save (or lose) by renting rather than buying is to use an online calculator. My favorite is Microsoft's at http://houseandhome.msn.com. Click on "Loans and Financing," then on "Calculators."

your daughter-in-law but find it difficult to live with them day in and day out. You may like the nice weather down south but miss your old friends up north. Or, you may find you love the change and find that it is a joy to baby-sit, it is easy to make new acquaintances, and the 85-degree temperature agrees with you. If so, then the decision to move is an easy one.

Cleaning Out

Moving, whether it is long distance or local, from a big house to townhouse, from the country to a co-op, provides you with a wonderful opportunity to do what we always put off: weed out. You now can get rid of those old skis and dusty hoola hoops.

You may find it easier to sort through things with the help of an adult child, your sibling, or a friend. Whether you do it alone or with someone, put on some lively music to lift your spirits and propel you into action. Begin with the room you think will be the least difficult to weed out and then go on to the more arduous ones.

Put these six large boxes in each room:

1. The definite junk box is for stuff that's in such bad shape that you wouldn't want even your worst enemy to have it. It goes in the garbage.

2. The charity box is for items someone else can use.

3. The think-about-it box is for things you should get rid of but just can't bring yourself to do so. It might be your husband's neckties, your grandmother's chipped teacups, and your high school prom dress. When you've weeded through the entire house, come back to all the think-about-it boxes. By then, you'll find it much easier to toss out most of the items they contain.

4. The uncertain box is for things you need to ask others about. Would your 30-year-old daughter like her old teddy bear? Perhaps someone among your nearest and dearest would like your

set of extra dishes. The hedge clipper might be just the thing for your brother-in-law.

5. The library/school box is for books in good condition. If you've saved magazines, call your public or college library to find out if they want back issues to fill in their collection.

6. The garage sale box is for items you think could sell. (See "Garage Sales" following.) It may be combined with your charity box.

For those items that don't fit into one of the six boxes, mark them with Post-Its, labeling them according to one of the five categories.

Don't try to go through the entire house in a day or even seven days. It's exhausting, both physically and emotionally, and a little goes a long way. When you're finished, call your favorite charity and ask them to pick up your charity boxes. Or, drop them off yourself. Make a list of what you are donating, the estimated value, and the date of the donation.

Garage Sales

After you've been the queen of clean and gone through your entire house, you may find that you have enough items to hold a sale.

Although garage sales are most popular when the weather is warm, they can be held indoors any time of the year. And if you're not in possession of a garage or a lawn, have one in your apartment, provided there are no ordinances against doing so. You'll find that someone will love your old ice skates, baby clothes, and fishing rods.

TEN STEPS TO A SUCCESSFUL SALE

1. Read your household insurance policy. Make sure you are protected should someone have an accident on your property. (Neighbors have been known to sue neighbors.) If you're a renter, you should not only check your renter's policy but also ask your landlord about his coverage.

Note: Many renters mistakenly think their landlord's insurance will cover their furniture and other possessions. Not so. You need to have your own coverage, known as HO-4. Most policies include liability coverage that covers any legal defense costs. The amount of liability protection varies but is usually three to ten times the amount of your personal property coverage. Cost: $30,000 worth of coverage will run $100 to $300 per year.

2. Check with your town hall. A growing number of localities require "assembly" or "business" permits for garage sales. The fees are minimal—$5 to $25—but the fine for not having a proper permit could be five to ten times that amount.

3. Plan ahead. Pick a date as far in advance as possible so you can put notices in local newspapers and on bulletin boards at churches, synagogues, libraries, grocery stores, and community centers. Resist including your phone number; if you do, you'll never get any sleep.

Three websites where you can post information about your sale are:

- www.yardsalesearch.com
- www.garagesalehunter.com
- www.pennysaverusa.com

Phrases that capture attention include "Everything Must Go," "More Than 500 Items," "Exceptional Antiques," and "A Three-Generation Sale." Three-generation sales are especially effective because shoppers know there will be a wide variety of items to look at—many of them old, interesting and valuable.

Mention if you're selling large items that require a truck or van to remove them. Your notices should also indicate if the sale will go on rain or shine or if there's a rain date.

Two-day weekend sales draw larger crowds than those held just one day or during the week. *Exception:* If you live in a city where people take off for the country on Fridays, run your two-day sale on a Sunday/Monday or a Thursday/Friday.

4. Join with neighbors. You'll get much more action if several of you hold a mini block sale. Joint deals not only attract more buyers and make for more impressive ads, but if you put everything in a central location, you and your neighbors can help one another when you need breaks.

5. Have plenty of change. Make a trip to your bank or ATM machine the day before. You don't want to lose a sale because you can't make change for a $20 bill. The recommended amount is 100 singles, $50 in $5 bills, $50 in $10 bills, and several roles of quarters. Then, only accept cash. Never take personal checks.

If you're accepting bids on certain items, keep a notebook for recording the potential customer's name, phone number, amount of their bid, and the best time to reach them. Have preprinted receipt forms for those who leave a deposit.

6. Serve cookies and lemonade. Free refreshments keep shoppers shopping longer, especially those who are hungry. Kids, even very young ones, can be put in charge of the stand because it doesn't involve handling money.

7. Set up a play area. Hire a teenager or grandparent to keep little children busy, reading books, playing games, drawing, or singing. This guarantees that their parents will poke through your wares at leisure, uninterrupted by little voices asking, "Mommy, when can we go home?"

8. Organize your tables. Put like items together. It makes shopping easier. Categories include clothing, toys, games, sporting equipment, small appliances, office equipment, books, records, CDs, collectibles, household items, jewelry, large equipment and appliances, and furniture and antiques.

Don't place the pricey stuff at the end of your driveway or at the entrance to the sale. Shoppers will turn away if it appears that you're items are too expensive or overpriced. All high-cost items should be next to where you will sit.

If you're selling jewelry, sunglasses, hair bows, scarves, hats, or neckties, have a mirror so people can see how lovely they look wearing your accessories. If you have a number of pieces of clothing, hang them on a portable coat rack or clothesline and be sure to set up a private trying-on area.

> **$TIP: Items are more likely to sell if they're up, off the floor or lawn, and easy to see and examine. It helps too if they are clean.**

9. Be cautious. Keep your money in a fanny pack. In other words, don't place money in a box on a table. And, lock your house. A yard/garage sale is often an open invitation to those less honest than yourself.

I also urge you to keep your pets in the house while the sale is going on. Just as not everyone is honest, not everyone loves parakeets, poodles, and pythons. You don't want shoppers to leave because they are allergic to cats or afraid of dogs.

10. Donate leftovers to charity. It's tempting, but don't stuff rejects back into your garage or closet. Keep in mind that you're moving. Instead, take them to your favorite charity. (Some charities will pick up substantial contributions.)

> **$TIP: Ask charitable organizations to which you are making donations for written receipts, on their letterhead, stating the dollar value of your donation. If you're asked to supply the value of your donation, don't inflate it. Check to see what similar items are priced for at area thrift shops. The IRS loves to come after exaggerators. If you itemize on your tax return, you can deduct the amount of your contribution.**

For More Help

"Charitable Contributions" (IRS Form 526) covers all the details (800-829-3676 or www.irs.gov).

Garage Sales 101, by Connie Carlson (Mouths in Motion, 2001) is full of practical information.

Moving to a Retirement or Gated Community

This section is for those of you who think you'd like to downsize and live where you no longer have to worry about putting on storm windows. Most retirement communities have a minimum age requirement—55, 60, or 62 are common. Gated communities do not. Both often come with golf, tennis, swimming, hiking trails, exercise rooms, and activity clubs. Many are located in college or university towns, adding classes to the list of things you can do for free or at a nice discount. You'll find it almost impossible to be lonely in such social environments.

You have many options:

- Resort communities. Located in resort-like settings and filled with facilities and amenities, these are ideal for widows with an active lifestyle. For example, Litchfield-Pawleys Island on Pawleys Island, SC, has golf, swimming, tennis, and biking trails and no minimum age requirement. On the other hand, Cherrywood Estates in Ocala, FL, which has a clubhouse, pool, spa, fitness center, tennis, billiards, arts and crafts, and dance classes, has a minimum age of 50.

- Active Adult Retirement Communities (AARC). These are age-restricted developments with an overall master plan. Many are self-contained cities with their own stores, hospitals, and security forces. The minimum age is usually 55. Some will not allow anyone younger than age 18 to live there permanently, although younger visitors generally can stay for up to a month.

  AARCs are made up of independent homes, cottages, condominiums, and apartments where people take care of themselves. They may have on-site swimming, golf, fitness programs, and classes at nearby colleges.

  The best ones encourage you to visit first. Del Web Vacation Getaway program, for instance, offers getaways at most of its 15 active adult communities in eight states (800-433-5932 or www.delwebb.com). Four nights at its Sun City Grand near Phoenix costs $300 to $400 for a one-room villa.

Note: Resort Communities and Active Adult Retirement Communities are sometimes grouped under the heading Independent Living Communities.

- Continuing Care Retirement Communities (CCRC). These provide different levels of residential living plus health care services and medical assistance when needed—all in a campus-like environment. Many women find they like the pleasure of living in a small attached home or apartment (known as independent living) and the comfort of knowing they can easily move to an assisted living unit or a nursing home when and if needed. You can usually opt for one to three meals per day. Local transportation, activities, and housekeeping are generally included in the cost.

  Some of the newer CCRCs have small golf courses, heated pools, fitness centers, libraries, branch banks, hair salons, pharmacies, religious chapels, organized daily activities, overnight trips, and opportunities for doing volunteer work.

- Assisted living facilities. Usually licensed by the state, these combine a residence with various types of support services. They are designed for those who need ongoing help with daily activities, such as bathing, dressing, and taking medication. Often part of a CCRC or nursing home, assisted living facilities provide 24-hour, seven-days-a-week supervision.

- Alzheimer's care facilities. These specialize in caring for patients with this disease or other forms of dementia.

- Nursing care facilities. These provide skilled nursing care to those who require it on a regular basis but do not need to be hospitalized. These facilities may be freestanding or part of a senior community.

FINDING THE RIGHT ONE

If you don't have a place picked out, there are plenty of sources that will lighten up the search process. Begin with the Retirement Living Information Center (203-938-0417 or www.retirementliving.com). Here you'll easily find more than 1,000 facilities described, ranging from those in resort settings (such as Scottsdale, AZ, and Fort Myers, FL) and college towns (Amherst, MA, and Chapel Hill, NC), to independent living and assisted living facilities and places for those with Alzheimer's and/or who need nursing care. Senior Resource (877-793-7901 or www.seniorresource.com) has similar listings. On both sites, a search by facility and/or by state will turn up the name, address, phone number, website (if available), and a brief description for each listing.

If you have health concerns, the American Association of Homes & Services for the Aging (202-783-2242 or www.aahsa.org) covers 5,000 plus not-for-profit nursing homes, continuing care communities, and assisted living facilities.

You can also contact some of the large retirement community companies for a list of their places and prices. Ask what arrangements they make for short-term, trial visits.

For More Help

For additional resources on housing and relocation, see also "For More Help" following "All about State Taxes" later in this chapter.

Adult 55+ Communities (877-55-ACTIVE or www.activeadulthousing. com) has active adult communities in New Jersey and Pennsylvania.

Covenant Retirement Communities (800-255-8989 or www. covenantretirement.com) has communities in California, Colorado, Connecticut, Florida, Illinois, Michigan, Minnesota, and Washington.

Heritage Communities (888-787-4663 or www.heritageseniorliving. com) has active adults and country club communities in Arizona, California, Colorado, Illinois, Michigan, Minnesota, New Jersey, New York, Oregon, and Virginia.

Marriott Senior Living (800-880-3131 or www.marriottseniorliving. com) has 125 communities in more than 25 states, including independent living and assisted living facilities.

U.S. Home Active Adult/Golf Course Communities (888-787-4663 or www.ushome.com) has country club communities in nine states including Colorado, Florida, New Jersey, Texas, and Virginia.

Webb Active Adult Communities (800-808-8088 or www.delweb. com) has 19 adult/country club communities in Arizona, Florida, Massachusetts, Nevada, New Jersey, and South Carolina.

TIPS BEFORE BUYING

- Go there. Once you've narrowed down your choice, visit the community, preferably staying overnight or at least in the evening as well as the daytime. You could also vacation in the area for a week or so to get a sense of what living there would really be like.

- Get the drift. Find out what the worst weather season is—how hot, how cold, how rainy, how snowy.

- Check the transportation. If you're going to be hanging up your car keys, make sure you can get around town. Does the retirement community have a free shuttle service to the library, bank, doctors' offices, ballpark, and the movies?

- Know the geography. Is there a nearby airport, train station, or bus terminal family and friends can use? How long a drive is it from your nearest child? The experts running Senior Resource report that 70% of Americans 65 or older live within one hour of one child. You don't want to be geographically isolated from the people who care about you the most.

- Find out about taxes. If the retirement community is in a different state, will you be paying more or less in taxes? Retirement Living (203-938-0417 or www.retirementliving.com) has continually updated information on taxes, state by state, plus links to each state's Department of Revenue.

- Study the rules and regulations. Retirement and gated communities, co-ops, condos, and many new housing subdivisions often have a homeowner's association that can exercise a great deal of control over how you use your property. These restrictions, known as Covenants, Conditions, and Restrictions (CC&Rs) may be enforced with the rigidity of an army drill sergeant or the kindliness of a gray-haired grandmother. Either way, you need to know what they are and make sure you're comfortable with them.

  CC&Rs typically restrict the colors you can paint your house, the colors of curtains or blinds that can be seen from the street, even where you can hang your laundry. Common regulations about size, style, or acceptability relate to a wide range of issues from installing basketball hoops in the driveway to running home businesses.

- Check maintenance fees. Homeowners' associations almost universally assess mandatory fees to cover maintenance of the common property. This can be expensive if the community has a pool or golf course. The board also may be allowed to raise the fees by a certain percentage every year to cover capital improvements. Be sure to calculate such costs into your housing budget.

Moving to a College Town

Living near your alma mater or someone else's can offer a very full life. Not only can you take classes day and night, but in most cases you have access to a library, a gym, tennis and squash courts, a swimming pool, perhaps even a golf course. Concerts, plays, football games, and great bookstores and museums beckon. Many college towns also have excellent medical centers.

COLLEGE TOWNS WITH RETIREMENT COMMUNITIES

Some of the many other college towns that have retirement communities near their campuses are:

- Amherst, MA: Amherst College
- Athens, GA: University of Georgia
- Bellingham, WA: Western Washington University
- Berkeley, CA: University of California
- Boulder, CO: University of Colorado
- Burlington, VT: University of Vermont
- Cambridge, MA: MIT and Harvard
- Chapel Hill, NC: University of North Carolina
- Charlottesville, VA: University of Virginia
- Lawrence, KS: University of Kansas
- Madison, WI: University of Wisconsin
- Northampton, MA: Smith College
- Oberlin, OH: Oberlin College
- Princeton, NJ: Princeton University
- South Hadley, MA: Mount Holyoke
- Stanford, CA: Stanford University
- Williamsburg, VA: College of William and Mary

An increasing number of Continuing Care Retirement Communities are linked to colleges and universities. They offer a choice of housing styles—independent living, assisted living, and nursing homes—all in the same site. Among the leaders in this category are The Village at Penn State in State College, PA; The Colonnades in Charlottesville,

VA (adjacent to the University of Virginia); Green Hills at Iowa State in Ames, IA; and Meadow Wood at Indiana University in Bloomington, IN.

You can also rent or buy housing near a campus. If you purchase a sufficiently large enough property, rent out rooms to faculty and students, adding to your monthly income stream.

Be sure to visit while college is in session.

All About State Taxes

The academic atmosphere and the weather are not the only climates to investigate when making a move. The tax climate is equally extremely important. State taxes vary dramatically, and different types of income are taxed at different rates. (Property and sale taxes can also take a big bite.)

STATES WITH NO TAX ON SOCIAL SECURITY BENEFITS

Alabama	Illinois	New Jersey
Arizona	Indiana	New York
Arkansas	Kentucky	North Carolina
California	Louisiana	Ohio
Delaware	Maine	Oklahoma
District of Columbia	Maryland	Oregon
Georgia	Massachusetts	Pennsylvania
Hawaii	Michigan	South Carolina
Idaho	Mississippi	Virginia

PERSONAL AND RETIREMENT INCOME TAX

You can avoid paying personal and retirement income tax if you live in one of the nine states that has no personal income tax: Alaska, Florida, Nevada, New Hampshire, South Dakota, Tennessee, Texas, Washington, and Wyoming.

In all the other states, personal and retirement income is taxed very differently. Tennessee, for example, does not tax salaries or pensions, but dividend and interest income from stocks, bonds, CDs, and the like are taxed at 6% if the amount is over $1,250 for an individual.

Other states also try to encourage new residents. Georgia, Louisiana, South Carolina, and Virginia exempt residents over a certain age from tax on some or all of their income from Social Security, pensions, and retirement accounts. If you move to Illinois or Pennsylvania, you'll find there's zero tax on income from Social Security, private pension, military pensions, public pensions, or withdrawals from IRAs or 401(k)s.

For More Help

AARP (800-424-3410 or www.aarp.org) publishes *Selecting Retirement Housing*, a free book filled with sound advice and helpful worksheets.

American Association of Homes and Services for the Aging (800-675-9253 or www.aahsa.org) publishes *Getting Started: A Look at Nonprofit Senior Housing & Care Options*, which lists 5,000 nonprofit nursing homes, CCRCs, assisted living, senior housing facilities, and community service organizations.

Assisted Living Federation of America (703-691-8100 or www.alfa.org) provides a state-by-state list of assisted living complexes throughout the United States.

BankRate (www.bankrate.com) posts a summary of each state's tax rules. Click on "Taxes" and then go to "State Taxes." The material is updated regularly.

Choose a College Town for Retirement, by Joe Lubow (Globe Pequot Press, 1999).

Continuing Care Accreditation Commission (202-783-7286 or www.ccaconline.org) provides information on its accrediting procedures, which are based on the facility's finances, health and wellness programs, services, and overall environment. There's also a state-by-state list of accredited CCRCs. Email the commission to see if a facility you're interested in has received accreditation.

Home Fair (800-557-2300 or www.homefair.com) has relocation information, average home prices, and information on the cost of living in various cities. The "Salary Calculator" enables you to compare the cost of living among different cities around the country. The "Community Calculator" helps you identify neighborhoods in different areas of the country that are demographically similar to where you are currently living.

Virtual Relocation (www.virtualrelocation.com) will help you compare the cost of living among different U.S. cities.

Moving Day

Moving ranks as one of life's most stressful occasions—not, of course, as stressful as death, as you well know, but it's certainly not easy. However, like many things in life, the more you know about it, the less expensive and troubling it will be.

BEFORE THE LOADING TRUCK ARRIVES

Step 1. Pick a licensed mover. Do not let your fingers do the walking through the Yellow Pages for this one. Instead, ask friends, colleagues, your real estate agent, or your new boss for recommendations. Then, call your state Department of Transportation to make certain the mover is licensed. You'll find the number as well as lots of helpful hints at 877-MOVING-U or at www.moving.com/moving/dot.asp.

Check too with your local Better Business Bureau to see if complaints have been lodged against a moving company.

It's somewhat of a plus if the mover is a member of a local group—a trade association, the Chamber of Commerce, the Kiwanis, or the Odd Fellows. And, those who are members of the American Moving & Storage Association (www.moving.org) have agreed to abide by published tariffs and a code of conduct that requires complete disclosure, written estimates, and participation in an arbitration program.

At Moving.com (877-MOVING-U or www.moving.com), every mover listed on their pages (search by zip code) has been prescreened for the necessary licenses and insurance coverage as well as for quality of service. The site has a customer feedback page, so movers who get numerous serious complaints are removed from the recommended list.

Step 2. Get written estimates. Note the word "written." The Better Business Bureau recommends getting at least three—and why not? They're free. Keep in mind, though, that an estimate is just that and not a guaranteed price. Nor can you get a binding estimate by phone or over the Internet. The mover needs to look over everything you want moved in person.

Before the mover arrives, separate what you're moving into three categories. (You don't have to physically separate these items but you must be able to identify them to the mover so that an accurate estimate can be made.)

1. Items you will pack
2. Items you want the mover to pack
3. Items going into storage

Be sure to show the mover absolutely everything you want loaded onto the van, including stuff in the basement, garage, and attic. And, don't forget any boxes shoved under your bed.

Step 3. Protect yourself. The price estimate is fraught with potential problems. Many otherwise brilliant people don't take time to note the different types of estimates:

"LADY, DO THESE STAY OR GO?"

The following items cause the most confusion for movers—that is, whether you're taking or leaving them.

☐ Lawnmowers   ☐ Wall-to-wall carpeting

☐ Humidifiers   ☐ Lawn furniture

☐ Washers   ☐ Barbecues

☐ Dryers   ☐ Bookcases

☐ Chandeliers   ☐ Portable swimming pools

☐ Venetian blinds   ☐ Ceiling fans

☐ Drapes   ☐ TV antenna or a satellite dish

- **Binding estimate.** Here the mover gives you a flat price that, allowing for a small percentage for potential change, binds both you and the mover. The final price cannot be higher than this figure unless you require additional services, such as the fact that the elevator isn't available in your old or new building or you didn't explain your building's moving restrictions clearly, like everything must go through the service door or that it's a walkup. Official acts of God that delay the driver can also add to the price, such as earthquakes, fires, floods, and hurricanes. Heavy traffic or severe road problems might also boost your bill.

  Find out, too, if the company charges a fee for making a binding estimate; some do.
- **Nonbinding estimate.** This is not really an estimate but really a price list. Nonbinding estimates are the mover's best guess, with the final price determined by the weight of your possessions for an interstate move or by the actual hours required for an in-state move.

TEN WAYS TO SAVE MONEY—AND HASSLE—ON YOUR MOVE

1. Do a clean sweep. Before you move, get rid of things you no longer need. Hold a garage sale, donate what doesn't sell to charity for a tax deduction, or give stuff away to family, neighbors, and friends. The fewer items you move, the cheaper the final bill.

2. Sell appliances. They're heavy and cost a ton to move, so if your stove, refrigerator, washer, dryer, or freezer are not new, sell them to the people moving into your old house or apartment. (Chances are that your new place will already have the major appliances in place.)

3. Do your own packing. But keep in mind, movers are liable for breaking any items they pack but not for the ones you wrap. You can also save money by getting your own cartons rather than buying them from the mover. Liquor boxes are strongest and not too big.

4. Don't pack aerosols or other dangerous substances. Doing so is illegal, and you could be hit with a heavy fine. Ditto for caustic drain cleaners, gasoline, charcoal starter, paint thinner, bottled gas, cleaning fluids, oil-based paints, matches, and ammunition. If they explode or start a fire you can forget about winning an insurance claim.

5. Rent a truck and move yourself. You'll probably have to rely on the help of friends and family but, regardless, check your homeowner's or auto insurance policies to see if rented trucks and your possessions are covered while moving. If not, buy coverage from the rental agency.

6. Negotiate. Moving is a competitive business. Although interstate movers must post their rates with the U.S. Department of Transportation, they also can offer discounts. However, they're not likely to volunteer this information.

7. Plan ahead. When using a pro to move locally, keep in mind that you're paying by the hour. So, reduce the time factor by stripping all

the beds and making certain there's a parking space for the truck at both your old and new house.

8. **Know the terms of payment.** Most moving companies require cash or a certified check, although some take some major credit cards. If you don't arrange for proper payment, the mover is legally allowed to put your goods in storage and charge you both storage and redelivery fees. So, have plenty of money in your checking account and if you need a certified check, get it during the week, unless your bank is open on weekends.

9. **Move off-peak.** Weekends and spring and summer months typically cost more.

10. **Keep all receipts.** If your move is job-related, some or all of it may be tax deductible.

> **$TIP:** If you have a nonbinding estimate and it turns out the final cost is higher than originally estimated—perhaps because your goods were heavier than anticipated or you decided to take the baby grand at the last minute—you'll be required to pay the original estimate plus 10% of the amount over that. The remainder will be due within 30 days after your goods are delivered.

- **Not-to-exceed estimate.** This quote is binding only for the mover. The final price cannot be greater than this dollar amount. If the move comes in under the estimated amount, you pay less.

Be sure you ask each mover you interview if they charge by the pound or by the hour and if there are extra fees for carrying things up a lot of stairs or for moving a piano, huge sofa bed, a car, or a pool table.

Step 4. Request each company's "annual performance report." Legally required, this includes the number of claims a company has received for damages, how often they were late delivering shipments, and how frequently they incorrectly estimated the final price of a move.

Step 5. Get an order for service. Once you pick a mover, you should receive a written order for service, estimating the cost of the move, any special services (packing and storage) involved, and the pickup and delivery dates. It should also include the method of payment. *Caution:* Don't accept a verbal estimate of dates or fall for the line, "We'll do this as soon as possible."

> **$TIP: The order for service is not a contract. You can cancel right up until moving day without being liable for charges.**

ABOUT MOVING INSURANCE

This is the number one problem area when it comes to moving, particularly if goods are lost or damaged.

There are four basic levels of insurance, sometimes known as "valuation coverage." A thumbnail sketch of each follows, but this is a complicated topic. If your mover doesn't explain each so that you understand what's involved, discuss the options with your own insurance agent.

1. Limited liability. Sometimes referred to as "released value," this is the minimum coverage required by law and is included in the base price you received from the mover. You don't have to pay a penny for it but, on the other hand, you barely get a penny should something go wrong—only 30 cents per pound (60 cents per pound if moving to another state) for anything that is lost or damaged. It's better than nothing, but that's about it. If your antique silver punch bowl ladle, which weighs less than a pound, is lost, you'll be lucky to get 50 cents. If a ten-pound stereo component, valued at $1,000, is lost or destroyed, the mover would be liable for no more than $6.

According to Moving.com (www.moving.com), if the truck disappears never to be seen again, the maximum you'll receive is $2,500. So, it seems pretty obvious that extra insurance is a good idea.

2. Declared value. Under this option, the value of your shipment is based on the total weight of the shipment times $1.25. A 4,000-pound shipment would have a maximum liability of $5,000. So, if you ship a ten-pound stereo component that originally cost $1,000, the mover would be liable for up to $1,000, based on the depreciated value of the component.

Also, under this plan, the mover is entitled to charge you $7 for each $1,000 of liability assumed for the shipment. So, the valuation charge for a shipment valued at $5,000 would be $35.

3. Lump-sum value. This type of coverage is similar to declared value coverage. If the value of your shipment is over the $1.25 per pound times the weight of the shipment, you may get additional liability coverage from your mover. You do this by declaring a specific dollar value for your shipment. (The amount you declare, of course, must be more than $1.25 per pound times the weight of the shipment.) You're also subject to the same valuation charge as in choice #2—that is, $7 per $1,000.

If you have items that are unusually expensive, you may wish to declare this extra value. You do so in writing on the bill of lading. You then pay a premium, which typically is less than 1% of the value covered.

4. Full value protection. Also called "full replacement value," this type of coverage guarantees that the insurance company will replace any item that is lost or damaged beyond repair with either a like item or a cash settlement. The cash settlement will be at the current market replacement value.

A key point to keep in mind is that unlike the other three options, depreciation of the lost or damaged item is *not* a factor in being able to determine replacement value. You'll need to ask your mover what the cost of this coverage will be.

Before buying extra insurance, check your renter's or homeowner's policy; it may already cover your move. If not, ask how much they would charge to insure your goods during the move and compare options and prices with those offered by the mover. If your employer is paying for the move, find out if any special insurance is available through your company.

Keep in mind that insurance from your mover will not automatically pay for any and all damage. You must be able to show that the mover caused the damage. So, take pictures of your antiques and breakables the day of the move, with the date noted on the snapshots or video.

Also, items in boxes packed by you are not covered unless the entire carton was damaged during the move—not so easy to prove, either.

Under all four types of coverage, moving companies are allowed to limit their liability for loss or damage to items of "extraordinary value," unless you specifically list these articles on the shipping documents. What's regarded as "extraordinary value"? Any item whose value is more than $100 per pound.

ABOUT THE INVENTORY LIST

Movers keep an inventory of what's being moved, noting any damage or unusual wear. Before you sign the inventory, make sure it lists all items and that each statement about their condition is accurate. Don't be shy; you have the right to note in writing any disagreement.

When your shipment is delivered, if an item is missing or damaged, your ability to recover money from the mover for any loss or damage is often depending on the notations made on the written inventory.

The inventory should be very specific. It should not, for example, state "office equipment" but rather IBM ThinkPad, Hewlett Packard

DeskJet printer, and four mahogany filing cabinets. And, if you have a Winslow Homer, don't sign an inventory that merely lists "one oil painting."

THINGS TO TAKE WITH YOU

There are certain items you should carry with you—one of the most important being the *bill of lading*. This order of service spells out the estimate, all terms of the move, the method of payment, any special services, as well as the pickup and delivery dates. You want to have it readily available until your shipment is delivered, all charges are paid, and every claim, if there is any, is settled.

Other items to have in your carry-along bag:

- Telephone number of the moving company

- Extra cash and/or traveler's checks

- Papers related to the sale of your old home and purchase of your new one

- Keys to your new home

- Your insurance policies and your agent's phone number

- Any medications you and family members require, including contact lens material

- Your best jewelry

- A child's favorite blanket or toy

- Important personal records and documents

- Backup copies of your computer files

Note: The contents of your bank safe deposit box should be carried with you or sent by insured registered mail to your new bank.

YOUR "OPEN FIRST" BOX

Mark this box with red tape and fill it with things you'll need the first night at your new home:

- Toothbrush and toothpaste, toilet paper, soap, and towels

- Sheets, pillowcases and one blanket per person

- Plastic cups, spoons, and plates

- Instant coffee; tea bags

- Can opener

- Several lightbulbs

- Pajamas, robe, and change of clothing

- Clock and telephone

- Basic tools: hammer, screwdriver, flashlight, masking tape, and pocket penknife

- Pet food and bowl

YOU AND THE MOVERS

A moving van driver, who wishes to remain anonymous, gave me three valuable tips:

1. Offer packers and movers coffee, cold drinks, and snacks. Even if they decline, it puts them in a positive frame of mind and they'll handle your things with greater care.

2. Some moving companies use pickup or temporary help, especially during the busy season. If anyone arrives on your doorstep and appears to be intoxicated, high on drugs, rude or totally incompetent, immediately call your lawyer and then the moving

company. Tell the moving company that you've already notified your lawyer.

3. When moving in/out of an apartment or condo, you must advise the building superintendent, doorman, and elevator man in advance. In many buildings, advance notice is a requirement or the movers will not be allowed in. (And you might want to tip these service people for their extra trouble in helping your move go smoothly.)

RESOLVING DISPUTES WITH YOUR MOVER

What if when the moving company is unloading your dining room table, they leave it momentarily on the driveway and one of the guys puts a carton on top of it, making huge long scratches on the mahogany surface. Or, three boxes of your favorite china are missing. Or, the actual cost is way over the estimate. Every woman's nightmare . . .

Be prepared. Anticipate trouble. According to the Better Business Bureau, the number of complaints against moving companies increases every single year. So, take a camera, notepad, and pen to your new house just in case you're faced with a problem. The more documentation you have, obviously the better your case.

When your shipment arrives, do not sign the driver's copy (which is the original) of the inventory until you have thoroughly looked over all your furniture and the exterior of all unpacked cartons.

Have all fragile items unpacked so you and the van driver can examine the contents.

And, check off the number of boxes on the inventory sheet with the number delivered. If any goods are damaged or lost, report the fact in detail on the van driver's copy of the inventory. Never sign this document until you're sure this is accurate. (The inventory is generally attached to the bill of lading.)

Ask the moving company for a claim form for lost or damaged items. You have nine months from the date of delivery to file a claim, but obviously it makes much more sense to file it immediately. Spell out the specific problem and estimate the dollar amount involved. The moving company must acknowledge the claim within 30 days, and they must either deny the claim or make a settlement offer within 120 days.

To bolster your case, get out that notebook and keep a chronological list of all the events involved, including the name of the moving company, their address and phone number, the names of all people you spoke with, the date, a summary of what the movers said, and the names of witnesses. Then make photocopies of all related documents and receipts.

Witnesses are critical. As soon as you sense a problem, ask a neighbor, your lawyer, accountant, or friend to witness what's happening. Comments by a witness (who should not be a relative) can be critical in any civil case or arbitration.

If the moving company does not respond to your complaint, call the Better Business Bureau in the town where the moving company is headquartered. The BBB's "Movers Plan" may be able to help you get action or go to arbitration. Details on the process are posted at www.bbb.org/complaints/moverule.asp.

Another course of action, if you are unable to resolve the dispute with the company or if the BBB can't get action, is to file a civil action to recover in court. Remember, however, that this is likely to be expensive, especially if you hire a lawyer. On the other hand, if your mover participates in a dispute resolution program, your costs will be significantly less if you go to arbitration.

Movers who participate in arbitration programs are required to tell you this *before* they accept your shipment. The entire process is done through the American Moving & Storage Association. For a complaint form, call 703-683-7410 or log onto www.amconf.org. This form asks for the bill of lading number and provides space for you to describe your complaint, describe your mover's response, and spell out how you believe your complaint can be resolved. You will also obviously need receipts, photographs, estimates of damage, and the like.

A few other points you need to know . . .

The mover is responsible for electronic items that don't work after the move only if there is clear evidence that the item was dropped or mishandled during the move. Again, take a snapshot.

You're legally obligated to pay for the move, even if you're claiming extensive damages.

Your bill of lading states the pickup and delivery dates. If the mover misses these dates, you can file a claim for your expenses—your hotel or motel room and food costs. Be certain to keep clear records and all receipts.

For More Help

Moving.com (877-MOVING-U or www.moving.com) has in-depth coverage of legal and technical details on resolving disputes.

The American Moving & Storage Association (703-683-7410 or www.amconf.org) has practical tips on moving with pets, plants, and/or children as well as taking care of specialty items such as electronic equipment.

Steiner's Complete How to Move Handbook, by Shari and Clyde Steiner (Independent Information Publications, 1999) guides you through the entire process, step by step. Its "Moving Company Tips and Traps" chapter is particularly important.

Hanging Up Your Car Keys

If you're moving to a retirement community or you've simply decided it's time to become a Miss Daisy and let someone else drive you around town, you're going to have to get rid of your car. If it's in relatively good shape, you can sell it to a used car dealer, sell it privately, or give it to someone in your family. If it's an old clunker, you can donate it to charity.

SELLING YOUR CADDY THAT ZIGS

If you sell the car yourself, you can probably make as much as 25% more than what a dealer would give, provided you follow these tips:

1. Clean the vehicle. Vacuum the interior and the trunk. Get clean floor mats. Take the car to a body shop and have the dents painted and the exterior washed and polished. Then, spray the inside with lightly scented air freshener.

If the oil needs changing, do so. If the tires are bald, replace them. If a light is broken, fix it. It's worth spending several hundred dollars to make even the oldest of cars sparkle.

2. Set the right price. You've got to offer a bargain in order to offset the goodies that car dealerships are offering, such as zero-percent financing, service contracts, and, in some cases, roadside assistance. So, don't overprice your car.

To arrive at a reasonable price, first check your model's listing in one of the official pricing guides: *The Kelley Blue Book* (www. kbb.com), *Edmund's Used Car & Truck Prices & Ratings* (www.edmunds.com), or *The N.A.D.A. Official Used-Car Guide* (www.nadaguides.com). You can also list your car for sale on the NADA site for a $40 to $70 fee. All three sources list the whole-sale price, which is the amount you might get in a trade-in, and the retail price, which is the price at which dealers usually sell used cars.

Two other sources for help in determining price are AutoSite (www.autosite.com), where you click on "Pre-owned," and Consumer Reports New & Used Car Service (800-232-3470 or www. CRCarPriceService.com).

Then take your car around to the used car department of several dealers. See what they'll give you and set a price somewhere between retail and trade-in.

3. Get your documents in order. Have your car service information and repair records available for inspection.

By law, you must reveal the car's mileage. And, in a great many states, you must also indicate what defects there are, including if the car has been in an accident.

4. Advertise. Begin by putting a "For Sale" sign in the car window, then tell friends, relatives, neighbors, and colleagues. At the

same time, place a classified ad in your area newspapers. Pick papers with the highest circulation and run the ad on Fridays, Saturdays, and Sundays, when more people have time to read the paper and look at cars.

In addition to giving the year, make, and model, your ad should emphasize the car's best features, such as low mileage, leather seats, CD system, four-wheel drive, or never been in an accident. Mention the number of cylinders in the engine, whether it has standard or automatic transmission, and if it's air-conditioned. End the ad with the phrase "Excellent Condition," followed by the asking price and your name (first name only!) and phone number. Do not put your address in the ad.

$TIP: Three online sites where you can advertise and also see what prices other people are asking are www.ThriftyNickel.com (the online version of the weekly classified ad newspaper), www.SmartCarGuide.com, and www.autoweb.com.

If no one (or only one or two people) responds, it's probably because your asking price is too high.

5. Be tough. Make sure you know how low a price you'll accept. Experts recommend that you go with the first realistic offer from a buyer with cash. In any case, don't let a "shopper" tie up the sale by giving you a deposit while "thinking it over." You're likely to miss out on a really serious buyer.

Serious buyers stand out from the "tire kickers" because they insist on test driving the car. But before you let them behind the wheel, ask to see their license, make sure it's current, and write down their name, address, and phone number. Always accompany a potential buyer on a test drive.

$TIP: If for some reason you cannot accompany a potential buyer on the test drive, ask him to leave his car keys with you.

Caution: Never allow someone who walked to your house to test drive your car, unless, of course, it's a neighbor whom you know well. If it's a first-time car buyer who took public transportation, you or a friend should be in the car during the test drive.

6. Make the transfer. Do not sign over the title to the new buyer until you have a certified check or cash for the full amount. Then, sign the back of the title. Many states require that you fill out an official Department of Motor Vehicle's bill of sale. You can download a sample bill of sale and receipt at www.auto-used-cars-for-sale.com. Click on "How to Sell a Car." Or get a standard form at your local stationery store.

7. Finally, take off your old plates and cancel your auto insurance. The buyer should have new plates ready to put on when he collects the car.

DONATING YOUR CAR TO CHARITY

If you've got an old Betsy that no one is interested in, you can donate it to charity. You won't get cash, but you will get a tax deduction equal to the car's fair market value. Among those that are IRS qualified are the American Cancer Society, Veterans of America, and the Salvation Army. Many churches, synagogues, and other religious groups also accept donated cars. Check with your favorite local charity. You may get lucky.

Unfortunately most charities don't want to be bothered with really old models. One that does, however, is the National Kidney Foundation (800-488-2277 or www.kidneynca.org/car_donate.shtml). It will pick up any car, running or not, as long as it's in one piece and has a title that can be transferred. Another source for out-of-favor cars is Car Donation Charities (800-851-7199 or www.cardonation-charities.org). They will tow away your non-running car, free of charge, and handle the transfer of ownership. Your car will be taken to a dealer auction where it will be wholesaled to an authorized automobile dealer. The dealer then repairs the car so it is mechanically sound and resells it.

Once you make arrangements with a charity, get three copies of the charity's estimate of your car's value—one for your records, one for the IRS, and one for your state return. The IRS requires written acknowledgment from the charity as proof of charitable gifts (of cash or property) of $250 or more. If the car is worth more than $500, you must also attach IRS Form #8283, "Noncash Charitable Contributions," and an independent appraisal (also deductible) to your tax return.

Bottom Line

Moving is a huge undertaking, and never an easy one, but often worth the effort. As Helen Keller wrote, "Life is either a daring adventure, or nothing."

Chapter Fifteen

LIFE AS A YOUNG WIDOW

God could not be everywhere, therefore he made mothers.
—JEWISH PROVERB

Like all parents, I'm sure you and your husband found raising your children together a great joy and also a bit of a challenge. Taking care of them on your own, of course, intensifies both the joy and the challenge. As lonely as you may be now that you are a single mother, you do have an immediate family—children you love and who love you. They bring a focus to your life that widows without children do not have. However, you now have more details to attend to, more responsibilities to handle, more things to worry about. Your own parents and in-laws, siblings, and friends along with your lawyer will help you take care of the tasks discussed in this chapter.

Naming Guardians for Your Children

Just as you wouldn't leave young children home without a babysitter, you shouldn't leave them without making provisions for their future. And that means updating your will and naming a guardian for your minor children. Few things in life are more important than choosing the best person to take care of your kids in case you die.

If you have not named someone to assume responsibility for your children, anyone can ask for the position. The court will consider all applications (if there are any) and then appoint a guardian—very often a relative but not necessarily the relative you would have chosen.

THE PERSONAL GUARDIAN

The technical process is quite simple: you name the guardian in your will. That guardianship lasts until your child reaches majority, either age 18 or 21, depending upon the state in which you live. This man or woman is officially known as the "guardian of the person." (There is also a "guardian of the property," whom we'll discuss later on.)

Here are the factors to consider when choosing a guardian. He or she:

- Must be an adult; over the age of 18 or 21
- Should have a very real interest in your children and their future
- Should be physically and emotionally able to handle this responsibility on a long-term basis
- Should have the time to devote to the task
- Should share your religious, moral, and ethical beliefs
- Should be someone your children really like
- Should live relatively nearby, unless you feel your children would not mind moving

If you have more than one child, you probably want your children to stay together, in which case name the same personal guardian for each child.

There are some situations, however, in which it makes sense to name different guardians for different children. If your children are far apart in age, for example, each may have formed different bonds with different members of the family. Or, if you have children from several marriages, different guardians may be a wise move.

Choose someone approximately your age. In most cases, attorneys do not recommend naming grandparents simply because they tend to be too old and you don't want your children to go through yet another bereavement experience. Of course, there are exceptions to this advice.

Talk to the potential guardian ahead of time. Make certain he/she is very, very comfortable with this serious and long-term responsibility. Do not pressure someone into saying yes. Then name an alternate, in case your original guardian becomes critically ill or dies.

A PERSONAL LETTER

Mothers have very strong feelings about how they want their children to be raised. I'm sure you have your own personal set of beliefs, what you think is right or wrong, and important or not important. You've undoubtedly thought about where you'd like your children to go to school, what their strengths and weaknesses are, and how much money you want them to have, both now and later on in life.

One way to address your parental wishes and aspirations is to write a letter, outlining how you want your children to be raised. Take care not to be too technical or detailed; you don't want to assign the guardian tasks or positions he/she cannot fulfill. However, your general guidance will be both helpful to the guardian and reassuring to you.

THE GUARDIAN OF THE PROPERTY

The person named to be your children's personal guardian might not be the best person to handle the money you leave to your kids. Or that person may not want to assume financial responsibility. Discuss this matter with your lawyer. He may recommend naming a second guardian known as property guardian, an individual professional money manager or a financial institution.

Or, your lawyer may suggest that you pass your assets on to your children in a trust. A trust spells out how you want the money spent—on books, tutoring, lessons, summer camp, college, and so on. A trustee can then write checks up to the limits set by the trust without having to ask for court approval.

Moving Back Home

Thomas Wolfe may have written that "you can't go home again," but thousands of widows have proved him wrong. Temporarily moving in with your parents or in-laws may be exactly the right thing to do. It may give your children an opportunity to get to know their grandparents, provide comfort and support for you, and be economically very sound.

Returning home also offers you and your parents a chance to develop a close, adult relationship, to enjoy one another as individuals. But it must be handled thoughtfully to avoid straining family relationships and even retarding or hurting your own personal growth.

Living harmoniously with your parents at this point in your life (and theirs) is contingent on many factors. Some you can control, some you cannot. But you can ease the way if you let your family know that you don't plan to stay forever and that you do plan to pitch in. That means cooking, shopping, gardening, doing the laundry, walking the dog, cleaning, and paying rent.

No matter how old you are, it's almost impossible not to feel like a little girl when you walk into your old room and eyeball the artifacts of childhood on the shelves and walls. It's easy to fall back into the role of a 12-year-old again, even though you may be a mother yourself. The best formula for success is to draw up some guidelines with your parents or in-laws, ideally before you move, covering these points:

1. **Room and board.** Decide together how much money you should contribute. If you have children, you obviously need to contribute more than if you are a widow without kids.

Of course, not all parents are willing to accept money from adult live-in children, but offer anyway. You may be unaware of their current financial needs. Perhaps they are earning less than when you were young, perhaps they're on a set income, or perhaps they're having trouble making ends meet.

2. Household chores. Make a detailed list. If you have children, include special assignments for them as well. Cooking and mowing the lawn should not be left solely to your mother and father.

3. Guests and friends. This is your parents' house, so make every effort to adjust to their needs and wishes. Discuss having friends—yours and your children's—visit. If your parents have been living alone since you went off to college or got married, they're not used to toddlers running about opening cupboard doors, youngsters jumping up and down, or teenagers feeling moody, even though they went through all of those things with you. If they treasure a quiet Sunday morning, try to preserve that for them. If you have very young children, make it a point several times a week to take them to the playground or the library or to do things with other children.

4. Child care. If one or both of your parents will be babysitting while you go to work, offer to reimburse them for their time. If the answer is, "We don't want you to pay," try to cover the extra expense of having the children in your parents' house in other ways: fill their gas tanks, give them gift certificates to their favorite store or restaurant, or stock the refrigerator. Your parents may start out being very enthusiastic and absolutely thrilled to have their grandchildren under the same roof, but they may also run out of pep. If you sense their enthusiasm waning, bring in a babysitter, cut down on your hours at work, or take your kids to day care several times a week.

Becoming a Working Mom

If you already have a job, you can skip this next section, although you might want to run down the list of companies that are especially "family friendly."

HOW MUCH WILL IT COST?

If you were not a working mom, you may find that you need to earn money now or that you simply want to develop the professional side of your life, working either part or full time. Before you head to the

THE WORKING MOM'S EXPENSES

Day care	$ _____
and/or . . .	
Babysitter, nanny, au pair	$ _____
Household cleaning	$ _____
Commuting	$ _____
Wardrobe	$ _____
Weekday lunches	$ _____
Takeout dinners	$ _____
Taxes*	$ _____
Total	$ _____

*Ask your accountant for a rough calculation of what your taxes would be given a specific salary. You will be hit with Social Security taxes, federal income taxes, and, depending upon where you live, state and local income taxes.

At the same time, ask your accountant about the Dependent Care Tax Credit. If you spend money on child care in order to work or to look for work, you can probably claim a credit against your federal income taxes. This credit is also explained in IRS Publication #503, *Child and Dependent Care Expenses*, available by calling 800-829-3676 or by logging on to www.irs.gov.

mall to purchase a navy blue interview suit, total up the costs of going to work. Then you'll know how much salary you need in order to more than cover your expenses—something that's best to realize before you start your job search.

THE BEST COMPANIES TO WORK FOR

Some professions, some companies, and some bosses are much more accommodating and understanding about the issues working mothers face.

Every year, *Working Woman* magazine lists the best companies for working mothers. For the full list, go to www.WorkingMother. com/100best.shtml. You can click through to the individual company's website to find out what family friendly programs are offered.

In some cases, you can also read about positions that are available and even apply for work online.

If you don't live near one of the top 100 companies, learn about family friendly companies in your area from neighbors and friends and by reading the local newspaper. Local career counselors and placement agencies are also well informed.

Forbes magazine has a slightly different annual compilation: the companies with the highest percentage of women employees. Among these companies are American Express, Capital One, Edward Jones, Lands' End, LensCrafters, Nordstrom, Paychex, Starbucks, and Wal-Mart. For the full list, go to www. fortune.com/lists/bestcompanies/ women.html.

THE TOP TEN COMPANIES FOR WORKING MOTHERS

Abbott Laboratories

American Express

Bank of America

Booz Allen Hamilton

Bristol-Myers Squibb

Colgate-Palmolive

Computer Associates

Fannie Mae

General Mills

IBM

Source: *Working Woman* Magazine

As a rule, the careers and companies most compatible with raising children are those that allow you to control part or your entire work schedule. Being your own boss or working for the right company means you can show up at music recitals, soccer games, and teacher conferences without a lot of hassle. Among the positions with above average flexibility are real estate agents, sales reps, freelancers, writers, painters, sculptors, those who own their own business, and those who work at home.

Careers that match your children's schedules likewise make life easier. Teaching is the most obvious one, but think, too, about being a teacher's assistant, a member of the school staff, an athletic coach, a tutor, a crossing guard, or a school bus driver.

Fast-track, highly pressurized positions, such as law, medicine, and investment banking are the toughest for working mothers, followed by jobs in which you must work long and hard hours, such as an on-staff journalist, a television producer or announcer, or a restaurant manager.

$TIP: When you go for an interview, ask about the firm's maternity leave even though it's unlikely you'll be having a baby soon. Knowing the policy will give you excellent insight into management's position about families.

FIVE IMPORTANT COMPANY PERKS FOR WORKING MOTHERS

1. On-site or company subsidized day care

2. Flexible spending account

3. Dependent-care account*

4. Flexible work hours

5. Gym or health center

*An account in which employees set aside up to $5,000 per year in pretax income to pay for dependent care for children, elderly parents, or other dependent family members. The money is considered a salary reduction and therefore is not taxed by the IRS. The funds are managed by the employer and used to reimburse the employee for eligible expenses.

WHERE THE JOBS ARE

Currently, there are nationwide shortages in nursing, teaching, day care (for children and seniors), health care, veterinary medicine, dentistry, and physical and occupational therapy. Continuing care and retirement communities as well as rehab centers and nursing homes are desperate for workers. Retail stores, restaurants, and fast food emporiums are continually looking for intelligent workers. If you can repair equipment of any sort, from TVs, toasters, and tractors to computers, cars, and china, you will get immediate work.

If you feel a little bit uncertain or insecure about being able to get work, just remember the wonderful advice of a popular bumper sticker of the eighties: "The best man for the job is a woman."

FINDING A JOB

There are many fine books on job hunting and resume preparation. You should probably read at least one. If it's been a while since you were a nine-to-five person, take a course in computer skills or the subject matter in which you're interested. Many new developments may have occurred in your field while you were car pooling, cooking, and cleaning. You want to be as up to date as possible.

In the meantime, here's a brief refresher course on landing a job.

- **Network.** Begin by talking to friends, family, and colleagues. Someone you know may know someone looking for a person with your skills and talent. In addition to reading the want ads in your local newspaper and professional journals, consider using a headhunter or a placement firm that specializes in your area of expertise or interest. It's also helpful to attend trade shows, conventions, and job fairs.

- **Use the Internet.** Seven places to look for jobs on the web include:

  1. CareerBuilder (www.careerbuilder.com) posts positions and offers excellent advice about resumes and interviews.

2. CareerShop (www.careershop.com) will email you when it finds a job match, based on information you provide. The "Salary Wizard" calculates how much you can expect to be paid based on the job and geographical location. For example, a librarian in New York City earns on average $41,181.

3. The Foundation Center (http://fdncenter.org) specializes in jobs in the nonprofit world.

4. HotJobs (www.hotjobs.com) has a sophisticated technology that lets job seekers control which employers see their resumes. Among its unique tools: a listing of temporary jobs, college positions, and a relocation survival primer.

5. KornFerry (www.kornferry.com) focuses on executive and professional positions.

6. Monster (www.monster.com) posts more than one million jobs per month including thousands of university positions.

7. The Idealist (www.idealist.com) covers paying jobs in the nonprofit world as well as volunteer positions and internships.

> **$TIP:** While you're online, read the qualifications for three or four positions in which you're interested. You'll immediately know whether your skills are up to date or if you need a little retraining. Knowing that you need to do spreadsheets on Power Point programs, have skills in Java, and speak at least one foreign language while you're logged on to an Internet site is much less embarrassing than finding this out when you're in an interview, sitting across the desk from an employer.

- **Get in the door.** If the company you'd like to work for doesn't have an opening or isn't offering you the position you want, consider taking a different job with the firm, even one on a lower level. Once there, you can demonstrate your abilities and commitment.

- **Be a volunteer.** Some companies and most nonprofit organizations have a number of unpaid volunteers and/or interns. If you're well-suited to the work, it's quite likely that eventually you will be hired for a paying position. Start with your local library, zoo, botanical garden, historical society, mayor's office, museum, school system, or college.

- **Think temporary.** Take short-term assignments. Fill in for someone who is sick, on vacation, or on maternity leave. It may lead to a full-time job, or you may find that you like the variety. More and more companies are using professional temps as workers in such fields as engineering, law, consulting, paralegal, and paramedics. Temping is no longer the exclusive province of office workers.

- **Look the part.** It's fine to be a soccer mom in a jogging suit and running shoes. But when you go for an interview, you should change your image slightly, even if you're applying for a job as a soccer coach. There's no need to become paranoid about your looks, but invest in a stylish-looking pantsuit or suit with a skirt. Wear it at least twice before going to your first interview. Then, get your hair styled and your nails shaped and polished. Leave your sense of outrageousness at home—at least until you get the job.

- **Prepare answers in advance.** Each interviewer has his or her favorite set of questions, but it's very likely you'll be asked about one or two of the following topics. Practice your answers in front of a friend who is supportive but will also critique your responses.

  - What was your last position?
  - What have you been doing since then?
  - What skills will you bring to our firm?

- What are your strengths?
- What are your shortcomings?
- What attracted you to our company?

- **Keep track of job hunting expenses.** Many of the costs of looking for a job are deductible from your taxable income under the category "Miscellaneous Itemized Deductions." However, not everyone on a job hunt qualifies for the deductions; you must be looking for a job in the same field in which you were previously working.

  Among the expenses that count: recruitment and agency fees, placing an ad in newspapers and journals, transportation to/from interviews, local and long-distance phone calls, and resume preparation, including typing, printing, and mailing. Be sure you keep receipts and detailed records documenting your expenditures.

  A word about transportation: If you are going to an out-of-town interview, your airfare, hotel, meals, taxi, and miscellaneous expenses are deductible. But don't try to turn your trip into a vacation. The IRS will be on your case.

For More Help

9 to 5 (800-522-0925 or www.9to5.org) is the largest nonprofit organization of working women, with local chapters in 50 states. The telephone hotline will answer your questions about job survival, unequal pay, family leave, sexual harassment, and other key issues.

BlueSuitMom (www.bluesuitmom.com) is designed for the executive working mother and provides help on how to balance work and family, run a business, search for a job, take care of a sick child, and other key topics.

TaxPlanet (www.taxplanet.com) covers tax-deductible expenses. Click on "Select a Link" and then "Job Hunting."

Paying for Your Child's Education

All parents have wonderful plans for their child's future and those almost always include college. But unless your husband left you extremely well off, you need to start thinking about college bills right away. The projected cost for a college degree is overwhelming; by the time your toddler enters the halls of ivy, tuition, room, and board for four years in an in-state school is expected to hit about $75,000. To get that amount by freshman year, if you're in the 28% tax bracket, you'll need to save around $200 a month, provided you get an annual return of at least 8%.

It may sound daunting, but this example cited above assumes you will be paying 100% of your child's college costs. Fortunately, your child can apply for a scholarship, tuition assistance, or low-cost student loans.

Caution: If you do plan on applying for financial aid, minimize the amount of assets held in your child's name. Most financial aid formulas require you, as the parent, to contribute 5.6% of your assets per year (while your child is in college) for tuition, but your child is required to fork over a whopping 35% of his or her assets.

Fortunately, there are a number of programs and savings plans to help meet those outrageous amounts. The key ones are covered below, but be sure to also read Chapter 11 on other types of investments and setting up a uniform gift to minors account. And, at birthday and holiday time, encourage family and friends to contribute to your child's education fund.

STATE 529 COLLEGE INVESTMENT PLANS

There are two types of state 529 plans: the College Savings Plan and the Prepaid Plan.

In the State 529 College Savings Plan, your money is invested in a special account, containing stocks, bonds, and money market funds or a combination of all three. Although the individual states administer the plans, the investment part is usually outsourced to an investment firm or mutual fund company. Plans differ from state to state, but here are the overall details:

- Earnings are exempt from federal taxes as are withdrawals as long as they go toward paying qualified college costs.

- Deposits can be made monthly or in a lump sum. Some plans require as little as $25 to open an account with subsequent investments of just $50.

- Plans have generous maximum contribution limits. In some states you can contribute up to $250,000 per beneficiary, at once or over the life of the investment.

- There is no age limit of the person you want to put through college—it could be you!

- The money can be used at any college, not just those in your state. When it is withdrawn to cover college costs, it is not taxed.

- You maintain control of the account. Although the money is for your child, he or she cannot withdraw the money and buy a BMW or take a trip around the world.

- Funds are treated as parental assets. Current financial aid formulas only count between 5% and 6% of parental assets when calculating a family's need figure.

- Grandparents can contribute. 529 contributions are considered "completed gifts" and are excluded from one's estate. Grandparents can also switch beneficiaries to other grandchildren.

- Beneficiaries can also be switched to first cousins.

- You can contribute to a Coverdell Education Savings Account (explained below) and 529 plans in the same year.

Caution: You are at market risk; if the funds you select go down in value, so will your account. And, in most plans, you can change investment options only once a year.

$TIP: You are not limited to joining your state's plan, but it might be wise. In over 20 state plans, part or all of your contributions are deductible from your state income tax.

In the State 529 Prepaid Tuition Plan (also called Prepaid Education Arrangements or PEAs), you lock in today's tuition price being charged at a public college or university within the state that is part of the plan.

There are two types of prepaid tuition plans. The Units Plan enables you to buy units of tuition. A unit might equal 1% of state college tuition or a set number of credit hours. A Contract Plan enables you to purchase one to five years of tuition.

Here are the upsides to prepaid tuition plans:

- You can generally contribute to either of the two PEAs in a lump sum or in installments.

- Earnings are guaranteed by the state government to at least match in-state tuition increases.

- Most programs allow funds to be transferred to private or out-of-state schools, but then you must pay the difference between the prepaid tuition price and the current price of the private or out-of-state school.

There are some downsides to prepaid tuition plans:

- They do not cover room and board, only tuition.

- Most, but not all, permit parents to transfer the money to an out-of-state school in case their child wants to attend a college farther away from home.

- Participation is often restricted to state residents or alumni of state colleges and universities.

- Your principal plus earnings may not cover tuition and account fees if your student goes out of state or to a private school.

- Pulling out of a plan usually results in stiff penalties and/or loss of interest.

- The plan can significantly reduce your family's eligibility for financial aid; distributions paid to the college are treated like scholarships and thus reduces the family's need figure on a dollar-for-dollar basis.

WHICH 529 PLAN IS RIGHT FOR YOU?

The College Savings Plan generally offers more flexibility in selecting a college. And, if you qualify for need-based aid, the federal formula will ask you to contribute less from the College Savings Plan than from a Prepaid Tuition Plan. However, your College Savings Plan is at market risk.

> **$TIP: To find out about your state's 529 plans, contact the National Association of State Treasurers (877-277-6496 or www.collegesavings.org). The website will link you to individual state plan administrators.**

THE COVERDELL EDUCATION SAVINGS ACCOUNT

Until recently this popular savings vehicle was known as the Education IRA. Now called the Coverdell, it allows you (or your family and friends) to sock away a total of $2,000 a year per beneficiary in a special account and then use the money—free of federal taxes—to pay for elementary, secondary, or college expenses. That means, if you have two children and you open two separate accounts, you could save a total of $4,000 per year. If you save $2,000 starting when a child is born, and your money earns 5% annually, you'll have over $54,000 when he or she starts college.

Here are the details:

- Contributions are not tax deductible, but the account grows tax-free.

- The child (a.k.a. the beneficiary) must be under age 18.

- Qualified expenses include tuition, books, fees, supplies, computers, and educational software.

- The account must be fully used by the time the beneficiary reaches age 30 or it will be hit with taxes and penalties. An exception: a child with special needs.

- If the beneficiary does not use the account, it can be transferred to a sibling. One rollover may be made per year.

- There are some income restrictions to make the full $2,000. Your adjusted gross income must be $95,000 or below. The contribution amount is then phased out between $95,000 and $110,000 for single filers.

- If your income is too high, you can gift the money to your child and then open the account.

- The money is counted as the student's assets, which can reduce your eligibility for federal financial aid.

- You can contribute to both a Coverdell and a 529 in the same year for the same child.

Some words of caution . . .

With this type of savings plan, the child is the beneficiary. When the child turns 18 or 21, the money is legally his or hers. That means you cannot control the funds forever.

If you plan on applying for financial aid, you'll want to minimize the amount of assets held in your child's name. Most financial aid formulas require you, as the parent, to contribute 5.6% of your assets per year (while your child is in college) for tuition, but your child is required to fork over a whopping 35% of his or her assets.

Finally, keep in mind that earnings in a Coverdell are not guaranteed; the account is subject to fluctuations that take place in the stock market and with interest rates.

THE ROTH IRA

You can withdraw money from your IRA to pay for college expenses without having to pay either income tax or the standard 10% early withdrawal penalty.

EE SAVINGS BONDS

These ultrasafe government bonds offer a low-risk way to save money for college. They are sold without a fee at local banks, through payroll deduction plans, and via the internet. They can be purchased for as little as $25, and the interest earned is exempt from state and local income taxes. The rate changes every November 1 and May 1. They are currently yielding 3.25%.

> **$TIP: If you purchase these bonds in your name and redeem them in the year you use the money for college tuition and your _adjusted gross income_ (AGI) is below a certain amount at that time), the interest will escape federal income taxes as well. That adjusted gross amount for a single filer is currently $57,600. However, that dollar amount may increase.**

For More Help

The College Board (www.collegeboard.com) spells out all the details on the State 529 College Savings Plan and the Coverdell account as well as information on finding federal aid and scholarships. Don't miss its financial aid calculator.

"Smart Saving for College 529 Plans and Other College Savings Options" is the best comparison of the various plans that I've seen. Check it out at the National Association of Securities Dealers (www. nasd.com).

Saving for College (www.savingforcollege.com) has several useful calculators.

T. Rowe Price (www.troweprice.com) has a five-step calculator that estimates how much you need to set aside if you have up to five children.

Help! I Am a Parent of College-Bound Children is available from the Investor Protection Trust (www.investorprotection.org/college.htm).

For information on using EE Savings Bonds to pay for college and how to buy them online, call 800-US-BONDS or log on to www.savingsbonds.gov.

Ernst & Young's Profit from the New Tax Law (John Wiley & Sons, Inc., 2001), Chapter 8, "Education," answers a number of common questions.

Paying for College without Going Broke, by Kalman A. Chany (Princeton Review/Random House; updated annually), is the definitive work on the topic.

Chapter Sixteen

LIFE AS AN OLDER WIDOW

Age doesn't matter unless you're a cheese.
—Billie Burke

Keep Billie Burke's advice in mind as you make major decisions about housing, work, or education. Plan as though you have time to do the things you want, the things that interest you. This *is* your new life; it is not a dress rehearsal.

Housing is at the top of the list of concerns for older widows. In Chapter 10, we discussed the pros and cons of moving and, if you decide to move, how and where to move. Two other topics you may be wrestling with are work and education.

Work for many women represents much more than income, although that's obviously very important. It means identity and status. It means being with people and having a sense of involvement. It means having a structure to the day and a reason to get out of bed each morning.

Going back to school may be a means to a job or to a better job, but it may also be an end in itself.

We'll discuss both in this chapter.

Where the Jobs Are

Smart companies realize that talent is not age related; it's related to what you can bring to the situation. That means you will want to market your strengths, but it doesn't mean you must stay with your former career. Many skills can be transferred to new positions and new lines of work. Or you can see this as an opportunity to do something that you really like and learn a new skill, like becoming a real estate agent, travel agent, certified financial planner, or lawyer. The possibilities are endless.

The following industries and stores favor hiring older workers because they dress nicely, show up for work on time, are polite, don't take phony sick days, and are dedicated to doing a very good job:

- Banks. Older workers are excellent as tellers and customer service reps.

- Bookstores. Older people are from a generation of readers. Bookstores as well as news and stationery stores value their expertise in literature.

- Child care. The growing number of working mothers has lead to a whole new industry, one in which older people bring patience, experience, and ideas.

- Florist and garden shops. Many hire older people part time to fill in during peak seasons, such as Christmas, Mother's Day, Valentine's Day, and spring planting.

- Hardware stores. Builders Emporium, Hechinger, and Home Depot all rely on older employees who have fix-up experience.

- Home health care. Demand is high for home health aides, physical therapists, companions, and people to prepare and deliver meals.

- Hotels. Over one-third of Day's Inn employees are 55 and older. The absentee rate is only 3%. Other chains, including the Marriott and Holiday Inn, also hire older people.

- Sewing and knitting stores. These stores require expertise and skills that older people often have.

- Tax return preparers. The IRS and accounting firms such as H&R Block hire people during tax times.

THE JOB SEARCH

Begin by reading the job-hunting tips I give younger women in Chapter 15. Many of them, networking in particular, have an ageless application. One of the advantages of being older, of course, is that you know more people and perhaps more people who can return a favor. Make a list of all your contacts. Call or email them telling them you're looking for work. If they suggest meeting, do so. If they don't, let it go.

GET HELP

If you're uncertain about what you want to do or how to go about it, attend a workshop or consult with a career coach. For example, the Five O'Clock Club (800-538-6645 or www.fiveoclockclub.com) is a private nonprofit outplacement firm with a nationwide network of career counselors. Membership is $49 a year plus $80 to $150 for optional one-on-one counseling. Career counselors will walk you through self-assessment techniques to help you prepare a resume, develop job search strategies, and manage your career.

If you do not live near a Five O'Clock Club, the National Board for Certified Counselors & Affiliates (336-547-0607 or www.nbcc.org) will find an individual career counselor in your area. You should also check your local community college; many offer career-counseling services to people who live in the area.

DOING A RESUME

The two most important factors in a successful resume is that it look appealing and that it is accurate, with no misleading facts, no serious omissions, no typos. Make it concise and detail your accomplishments, rather than just list the various jobs you've held.

If you're concerned about revealing your age on the resume, career experts recommend that you simply omit education dates and instead emphasize the last ten years. You can fold the rest into a short paragraph called "Other Experiences." Don't bother to include any experience that's unrelated to the type of job you're seeking.

Put three to four sentences at the top of the resume, focusing on your most outstanding qualifications. Then prepare two types of resumes, one that can be emailed (which many companies now prefer) and another that can be sent by regular mail. With the email version, it's important to keep all the lines of copy flush left. Email it to yourself to make sure it comes through in okay shape. Unless you are asked specifically to do so, do not send your resume as an attachment. Many employers do not open them because of the likelihood of a virus.

USE A TEMP AGENCY

According to the National Association of Temporary Services, some 260,000 retirees are working as temps.

> **$TIP: If you work as a temp, you can get around the fact that Social Security benefits are cut when annual wages are over $11,520 for someone under age 65. When your income reaches that dollar amount, simply delay going to work until next year.**

The following agencies actively use older people. Most offer free training to those who register. Manpower, for example, teaches computer skills and office organization. Check your phone book first for a local listing; if there is no listing, then call the company's headquarters or check the website as given below.

- Talent Tree, Houston, TX: 800-999-1515 or www.talenttree.com

- Kelly Services, Troy, MI: 248-362-4444 or www.kellyservices.com

- Manpower Inc., Milwaukee, WI: 414-961-1000 or www.manpower.com

- Olsten Corp., Melville, NY: www.olsten.com

- Randstad, Atlanta, GA: 888-RANSTAD or www.randstad.com

The group's trade group, the American Staffing Association (703-253-2020 or www.staffingtoday.net), in Alexandria, VA, will also refer you to a local agency.

AT THE INTERVIEW AND AFTERWARD

Realize in advance that you may be interviewed by someone who is young enough to be your son or daughter, so don't make a big thing about your age or the interviewer's age. Resist playing mother and saying, "Oh, you look so much like my daughter." Instead, focus on the three E's, being energetic, enthusiastic, and engaging. Point out that you can work intensely and you love a challenge. If you run marathons, play tennis, swim, or are a chess master, quietly work these details into the conversation. Although you should wear something that doesn't date you (like your old college pleated skirt with knee socks), don't select an "in" outfit that looks attractive only on a skinny 25-year-old. Keep your age and body shape in mind.

And remember, interviewers always remember a handwritten thank-you letter.

IF YOU'RE DISCRIMINATED AGAINST

It is unlawful to be turned down for a job because of age, if you're 40 or older. If you feel you've been discriminated against because of age, take action! Call the Equal Employment Opportunity Commission at 800-669-4000. They will conduct an investigation that could result in a settlement between you and the company or in filing a lawsuit.

Setting Up Your Own Business

You may decide this is a good time in life to start your own business. Ideally, it should be based on expertise you already have. One of the least expensive routes to take is to become a consultant, working from a home office. Some other suggestions include:

- Appliance, car, computer, printer, or fax repair

- Bill paying, letter writing

- Catering

- Child or elder care

- Computer programming and management

- Delivery or messenger service

- Freelance writing and editing

- House-sitting and house-cleaning

- House repairs

- Lawn and garden care

- Newsletter publishing

- Pet care

- Research and clipping service

> **$TIP: You will be able to deduct some of your office expenses, so be certain to keep accurate records and all receipts.**

For More Help

AARP (800-424-3410 or www.aarp.org/working_options/webresources. html) offers job resources for older workers. Also check out their *Working Options: How to Plan Your Job Search, Your Work Life* (www.aarp.org).

Experience Works (703-522-7272 or www.experienceworks.com), funded by the federal government, provides counseling, training, and employment services for older workers.

Office from Winstar (www.office.com) has free information on 150 industries and professions.

Operation Able (202-255-4230) is a nonprofit organization that helps older Americans go back to school, work, or volunteering. Check your local phone directory or contact headquarters for the nearest outlet.

The Senior Environmental Employment Program (202-260-2574 or www.epa.gov/ohros/see/brochure/) places retired and semi-retired people 55 and older in programs with the Environmental Protection Agency.

How Work Affects Your Social Security Benefits is free from your local Social Security office or from www.ssa.org.

Going Back to School

The news is full of stories about older women returning to school to complete their bachelor's degree, get a master's degree, or even achieve their childhood dream of becoming a doctor or lawyer. If this is the path you wish to take, begin by investigating courses at an institution near your home.

More than 24 states now have legislation mandating that publicly supported state colleges offer discounted tuition to senior residents. For example, Pennsylvania State University's "The Go 60 Program" allows state residents 60 or older to enroll in many degree programs for half of the regular tuition. A number of Illinois state universities invite Illinois residents 65 or older who have annual incomes under $12,000 to attend classes for free. Your state may offer something similar. I suggest you begin your search by reading *Never Too Late to Learn: The Adult Student's Guide to College,* by Vicky Phillips (Random House, 2002). It offers practical advice on picking a school and getting admitted, juggling your family and school life, and studing. The Appendix lists institutions that welcome seniors as well as long-distance study courses.

If you're not quite so serious and you simply want to take a class or two, now and then, check with your local school, museum, and Y about adult education classes. For example, the YMCA's Active Older Adults Program (888-333-9622 or www.ymca.net) has courses on health and wellness designed for those 55 and older. Although they are available across the nation, not every Y has them. If you want to learn how to use a computer or different types of software,

Senior Net (800-747-6848 or www.seniornet.com) has 190 learning centers throughout the country. It costs $30 to join the group and then $20 to $40 for an eight-week course. You must be 50. If you'd like to learn something new and fun in an interesting setting, check with Elderhostel (877-426-8056 or www.elderhostel.org). This non-profit offers learning trips and adventures in the United States and overseas for people 55 and older. You stay in university dorms or inexpensive hotels while studying. AARP (877-731-6941 or www.aarp.org/learn) has partnered with Fathom, a consortium of leading universities around the world, to offer a series of online courses in the arts and humanities, health and science, history, and personal finance. Some are free; others range from $45 for a two-session class to $600 for an extended course for college credit.

PAYING THE TUITION BILL

You may be tempted to put off going back to school because it's expensive. And it is. However, there are many sources of financial and private aid available to older women. These scholarships and grants just don't receive as much press coverage as does undergraduate aid. I recommend you begin with your employer. Many pay all or part of an employee's tuition, especially if the coursework helps advance your skills. Then, run through the following list:

• Back to College (714-447-0734 or www.back2college.com). Regardless of your focus, begin with this very comprehensive source. It not only has a hard-to-find list of programs that will give women academic credit for their life, business, and military experience, but it also connects you with a number of internships and online educational programs. Experts will answer your personal questions. You may want to order *Scholarships for Re-Entry Students* for $14.95 (includes shipping and handling).

• Professional organizations. Many offer aid for students, including adult students, who enter certain fields. They include the American Association of Law Libraries (312-939-4764 or www.aallnet.org/services/scholarships), the National Federation of Paralegal Associations (816-941-4000 or www.paralegals. org/choice/2000west.htm), the American Society for Mechanical Engineering (212-705-7375 or www.asme.org), and the American Dietetic Association (www.eatright.com/scholelig. html).

- Other professional fields. If you have a particular field in mind other than the ones mentioned just above, check with www. scholarly-societies.org for a list of many professional organizations that offer women financial help.

- Fin Aid (www.finaid.org). The home page has excellent coverage on basic financial aid with links to material on the federal tax credits. Type in "Older Students" in the search box and you'll be directed to specific advice and potential sources of money.

- Sallie Mae, College Answer (800-239-4268 or www.salliemae. org). The Federal Stafford Unsubsidized Loans, available for independent students, range from $6,625 to $18,500 a year.

- The Foundation Center (800-424-9836 or www.fdncenter.org). This has information on funds available from a large number of foundations. The center operates free libraries you can visit in New York; Washington, DC; Atlanta; Cleveland; and San Francisco.

- The Business & Professional Women's Foundation (202-293-1200 or www.bpwusa.org/content/bpwfoundation/scholarships) has career advancement scholarships for women who are at least 25 and want to upgrade their skills, train for a new career, or enter or reenter the workforce.

- Talbots (www.talbots.com). Through its Women's Scholarship Fund, the company gives five women $10,000 each and 50 women $1,000 each to pursue their undergraduate degree. They are limited to women who earned their high school degree or GED at least ten years ago.

- The American Association of University Women Educational Foundation (800-326-AAUW or www.aauw.org). This is one of the largest sources of funding for graduate women, teachers, those who are activists in their local communities, those who are at a critical junction in their careers, or those who are working in fields in which women are underrepresented.

- Soroptimist International (215-557-9300 or www.soroptimist. org). This business group's Women's Opportunity Grants program provides cash grants for head-of-household women seeking to improve their economic situation through additional training and education.

- Women's colleges. For a list of schools with special programs for older students, go to www.swordsmith.com and click on "Adult Student's Guides" and then on "Women's Programs." You may want to purchase their book, *The Adult Student's Guide* (Grossman and McBar) for $18.95.

ABOUT DISTANCE LEARNING

If you're confined to home or are working nine to five, getting to a college campus is not easy to arrange. But thanks to the Internet and other technology, you can take courses while sitting in your kitchen or bedroom. The phenomenon is so large that it's been given its own name—distance learning—replacing to some degree the old-fashioned correspondence course. International Distance Learning Course Finder (www.dlccoursefinder.com/us/stufaq/htm) will help you locate various ways to take a course at your own pace from home, including using video tapes, hooking up to satellite TV, taking the old-fashioned correspondence courses, and applying to e-schools. Search by subject matter, institution, or country. Two additional sources for information on distance learning are Mapping Your Future (www.mapping-your-future.org/features/distance.htm), which also will help you define your career goals, and Fin Aid, mentioned above.

Bottom Line

Being a student again, especially if you've been away from formal learning for a while, can be quite daunting. If at any time you feel discouraged, keep in mind the old Chinese proverb: "A journey of a thousand leagues began with one step."

Chapter Seventeen

YOUR NEW SOCIAL LIFE

He travels the fastest who travels alone.
—Rudyard Kipling

You probably thought it would never happen. You probably thought you would never feel like socializing again—connecting with old friends and meeting new ones. But eventually you do feel this. And, although it won't be the same as when you were part of a couple, it's important to get back into the swing of things—when you are ready. Doing so can put a strain on your budget, yet there are many ways to enjoy life without spending a fortune. We'll start with one of the activities Americans enjoy most: dining out.

Dining Out on a Budget

One of the nicest ways to stay connected with family and friends and to reduce loneliness is by dining together. But, as you know, it can be very expensive. Here are some ways around fancy meals at fancy prices.

I know several groups of women who meet for breakfast at their local coffee shop or pancake house. Those who are not working find it gives them a reason to get out of their bathrobes each morning; those who are working enjoy discussing the morning news with other women. Some of them combine it with a healthy walk. Breakfast, of course, is one of America's best bargains.

You can also take advantage of the early bird dinner specials, but dining at 5:00 P.M. may not be your thing. An alternative is to join a nationwide discount-dining program. Annual fees run around $50. Before signing on, make sure at least four restaurants that you like are in the program and that you will earn back the membership fee. Here are two programs to check out:

- **Transmedia/iDine** (800-438-9013 or www.idine.com) takes 25% off meals, beverages, tax, and tip.

- **In Good Taste** (800-444-8872 or www.igtcard.com) takes 25% off meals and retail purchases at certain establishments.

Here are some other dining out tips:

1. Dine out only for a reason. Save eating at expensive restaurants for special occasions. And, set a per week or per month limit on how often you'll leave your own kitchen at mealtime.

2. Drink at home. Alcoholic beverages in restaurants are always expensive. Invite friends to join you at home for cocktails and then go on to the restaurant.

3. Drink slowly. If you enjoy having a drink in a restaurant, order just one. If you're with a group, order a carafe of the house wine.

4. Eat ethnic. Mexican, Chinese, Thai, Japanese, Indian, and Pakistani restaurants are almost always a third less than American or Continental fare.

5. Skip the starter. You'll save a quarter of the price of a meal if you bypass the appetizer. Ditto on the dessert. Or, share a dessert. You'll half not only the price but also the calories.

6. Look for specials. Take advantage of lunch, brunch, pretheater dinner, and a prix fixe meal—all less expensive than a regular dinner.

7. Order from the middle of the menu. You don't need to have imported caviar, filet mignon, the flaming dessert, and the exotic mixed drink.

8. Play accountant. Always add up the check. Interestingly enough, most restaurant errors are in the restaurant's favor, not yours.

9. Get a doggie bag. Doggies bags have become chic even at the most expensive New York and Los Angeles restaurants.

Concerts, Museums, and Plays

Call your local museum, concert hall, and theater to inquire about days or evenings when admission is free or reduced. Most also have discounts for older adults. And ask about being an usher; you'll be able to see the performance for free while meeting other culture-loving ushers.

You can find out about more money-saving entertainment possibilities around the country at www.culturefinder.com. The site contains information on 300,000 theater, music, opera, dance, and visual arts events in 1,300 plus cities. Search by date or location or type of event. Tickets, often at reduced rates, are also sold at this site.

The Library

It may have been a while since you visited your public library. If so, you're in for a nice surprise. Libraries have gone beyond books and magazines. They now have books-on-tape for that long trip to visit your grandchildren, videos of movies you missed, and CDs to keep you up to date. Many also have computers with internet access as well as free lessons on how to use software. And, don't feel you must limit yourself to what is on the shelves; interlibrary loan makes the collections of far-reaching libraries available to all readers. Your library may also sponsor lectures, readings, and day trips and tours for "friends" at reasonable prices.

Travel

Women traveling alone is one of the fastest growing segments of the industry. That's good news for you because it means you'll find many trips, hotels, and cruises are now catering to women. If you are an "older" woman, you'll find you can also get excellent discounts.

Most likely the first bit of traveling you do after your husband's death will be to visit family or close friends. I want to make sure you don't overpay, so please take a quick look at these special rates. Then we'll go on to talk about taking major trips and vacations on your own.

DISCOUNTS FOR OLDER WOMEN ON THEIR OWN

Most hotels and motels offer seniors 10% to 15% off regular rates. Amtrak gives 15% off to those age 62 and older, and various bus lines, such as Greyhound (through its Seniors Club), have discounts starting at 10% for those age 62 and older. But you must ask for these discounts since they often won't be automatically offered.

Membership in American Automobile Association (AAA) or the American Association of Retired Persons (AARP) also entitles you to a number of travel benefits and discounts. So when booking a plane or train ticket or making a hotel reservation, always mention all your memberships as the reservationist may not remember to ask you. You'll find that some hotel chains offer even better deals than the AAA or AARP discounts as this sampling indicates:

Chain/Phone Number	Discount
Canadian Pacific Hotels: 800-441-1414	Up to 30% off for AARP members
Choice Hotels (Clarion, Comfort, EconoLodge, Rodeway, Quality, Sleep Inn): 800-424-6423	Between 15% and 30% off with an advance reservation

Day's Inn: 800-329-7466	At age 50, you can join the September Day's Club (free) for 15% to 50% off, plus 10% off at participating restaurants and gift shops
Hilton: 800-445-8667	If you're 60 and pay $55 for membership in the Senior HHonors program, you get up to 50% off
Howard Johnson: 800-446-4656	Get 10% to 30% off if you belong to AARP. If you are not a member, but you are age 55, get 15% off.
Marriott: 800-228-9290	Discounts vary by hotel
Radisson Hotels: 800-333-3333	The Senior Breaks program gives discounts for those age 50 and older that average 20%
Ramada: 800-228-2828	Free membership in Club Ramada, available at age 55, gives you up to 20% off
Swissotel: 800-63-SWISS	Varies by hotel

AIRLINE DEALS

Airline prices and policies are in a continual state of flux so, when you book your next ticket, ask if there are discounts for seniors or for two people traveling together, or if the airline offers coupon booklets entitling you to a free flight. Here is a sampling of some of the discounts available:

- America West's current range of discounts includes 10% off on most fares for those age 62 and older and one companion.

- American Airlines has a senior discount coupon booklet plus 10% off for those age 65 and older who book 14 days in advance.

- Continental's Senior Club ($75 per year) members get 15% to 20% off; non-club members get 10% off if they are age 62 or older.

- Delta offers coupon booklets for those age 62 and order.

- Frontier has a 10% off policy for those age 62 and older and one companion.

- Northwest gives 10% off leisure fares to those age 65 and older.

- United offers 10% off for those age 65 and older.

- US Airways has various discounts for AARP members.

RENTING OR SWAPPING YOUR HOME

Why let your house or apartment sit empty while you're traveling or going back to school? Renting it will help cover the cost of your trip or tuition and at the same time give you a sense of comfort knowing that it's occupied. You must, however, be prepared for some wear and tear—a glass may be chipped, a chair cushion stained, or a rug torn.

If you live in a condo, co-op, or gated community, check first with your board. You may not be allowed to rent, or you may be able to rent only for a certain length of time. Many require that the property owner's committee interview prospective short-term renters.

Then start networking with friends, neighbors, and colleagues. They may know someone looking for a place to stay in your area. Next check with local real estate brokers. Although you'll have to pay the agent a fee, the agent will be on the scene in case something goes amiss, such as the air-conditioning failing or the refrigerator not working.

You can also use a home exchange service that will help you trade your place for someone else's. Two firms that have been in business for a number of years are HomeExchange (800-877-8723 or www.

homeexchange.com) and World Wide Travel Exchange (888-205-3315 or www.wwte.com).

> **$TIP:** Whether you rent or exchange your house, put your valuables in a locked closet or room and take your prized silver and jewelry to your bank safe deposit box.

VACATIONING ALONE

You undoubtedly spent most of your vacations with your husband, and traveling without him may seem daunting, awkward, and, of course, expensive. But vacationing need not, in fact should not, come to an end. You don't want to become a recluse. Of course, the first time you venture out alone will not only be different, but probably difficult, accompanied by many bittersweet memories. One way you can ease back into the experience is by traveling with a group. If you don't have family or friends able to go with you, join a specialized travel group.

A handful of companies offer something called the "guaranteed share" rate; they give the lower double-occupancy rate to those willing to share a room or cabin with another woman. In many cases, if the company cannot find a roommate, you will be given a double room or cabin for the price of a shared one.

Among the companies that offer a guaranteed share rate for older travelers are:

- ElderHostel (877-426-8056 or www.elderhostel.org) is a non-profit organization that provides extraordinary learning adventures for people 55 and older. It has hundreds of programs each year in more than a hundred countries as well as intergenerational trips designed for grandparents, parents, and grandchildren. Some of its trips are on ships and barges that turn into floating classrooms.

- Grand Circle Travel (800-959-0405 or www.gct.com), which has been around since 1958, offers easy-paced trips all around the world.

- Overseas Adventure Travel (800-873-5628 or www.oattravel. com), which has been in business for more than 25 years, specializes in taking small groups (10 to 16 people) to "discover the road less traveled." Many trips are designed with the older traveler in mind.

- Saga Holidays (800-343-0273 or www.sagaholidays.com) has international and domestic trips for people 55 or older as well as its own cruise ship, the *Saga Rose*. It also has more than a dozen European tours with single-room accommodations at no extra charge.

- Solo Flights (800-266-1566) arranges trips for the single traveler, while its Mature Tours division has packaged trips designed especially for those over age 50. Its most popular destinations are London, New York, Costa Rica, Spain, Portugal, Morocco, and Australia.

Other companies and cruises that will match you with a roommate but are not focused on any specific age group are:

- Carnival Cruises: 800-227-6482 or www.carnival.com

- Club Med: 800-258-2633 or www.clubmed.com

- Cosmos Tours: 800-241-9843 or www.globusandcosmos.com

- Royal Caribbean Cruises: 800-327-6700 or www.royalcaribbean. com

- Trafalgar Tours: 800-457-6891 or www.trafalgartours.com

Sometimes single supplements are waived altogether on organized trips. This typically happens when a tour or cruise is not sold out. You can find them listed in *Connecting: Solo Travel Network,* a bimonthly newsletter (800-557-1757 or www.cstn.org).

TRAVEL CLUBS FOR WOMEN

Yet another way to find people to travel with is to join a club. These following three are for women only:

1. Women Traveling Together (800-795-7135 or www.women-traveling.com) runs long weekend getaways and other trips in the United States, Canada, and Europe plus a number of spa retreats. The average age is 40 to 65. Eighty percent come on the tour alone and are matched with other solo women travelers.

2. Explorations in Travel (802-257-0152 or www.exploretravel.com) has 18 years experience in leading trips for women over age 40 to Europe, Latin America, the South Pacific, and the American northwest and southwest.

3. The Women's Travel Club (305-936-9669 or www.womenstravelclub.com), founded in 1992, has special trips and cruises worldwide as well as spa packages.

TRIPS WITH A FOCUS

There are countless organizations and associations that cater to special interests or groups. Here are just a few of the options:

• Study gardens. The Litchfield, CT–based Expo Garden Tours (800-448-2685 or www.expogardentours.com), in its fifteenth year, has trips to the world's leading public and private gardens, with gardeners, horticulturists, and other experts accompanying each outing. In addition to trips throughout the United States, they go to Holland, France, Ireland, Italy, South Africa, and New Zealand.

• Be a farmer. Spending a weekend or week on a working farm can be delightful. Pennsylvania Farm Stay (888-856-6622 or www.pafarmstay.com) has details about 25 working farms located throughout the state that welcome guests and invite them to share in the farm chores (a fun choice if you have grandchildren).

- Go to summer school. The Senior Summer School (800-847-2466 or www.seniorsummerschool.com), which has been in business for 16 years, combines scholarship and sightseeing with two-week college sessions. Courses include political science, current events, literature, art appreciation, music, and philosophy. Social events, movies, live entertainment, some sightseeing, meals, and accommodations are included. Courses are available throughout the United States including La Jolla, Los Angeles, Madison, New York City, San Diego, and Santa Barbara.

- Volunteer. The nonprofit Oceanic Society (800-326-7491 or www.oceanic-society.org) has projects to save endangered species. Volunteers receive onsite training, and no experience is necessary. Global Volunteers (800-487-1074 or www.globalvolunteers.org) has projects in 18 countries and the United States. You can teach children in Romania English or help the Navajos make their buildings handicap accessible. Trip fees are tax deductible.

- Get in shape. If you enjoy physical challenges, Adventure Women (800-804-8686 or www.adventurewomen.com) has outdoor trips to the Banff National Park, to the Grand Canyon, and along the Lewis & Clark Trail among other destinations. Trips are ranked from easy to strenuous. Chicks with Picks (970-626-4424 or www.chickswithpicks) has beginner, intermediate, and advanced ice climbing in Colorado and New Hampshire. Luna Tours (877-404-6476 or www.lunatours.com) operates women-only biking tours in the United States and Canada.

- Learn history. Several companies run reasonably priced tours to key battlefields. IMM Tours (800-250-4988 or www.immhistory.com) visits the American battlefields of World War I, stopping in Paris, Verdun, and Reims. Military Histori-

cal Tours (800-722-9501 or www.miltours.com) focuses on
World War II European and Pacific theaters, while Matterhorn
Travel (800-638-9150 or www.matterhorntravel.com) covers
the Civil War battlegrounds.

- Take cooking lessons. Tuscan Way (800-766-2390 or www.
  tuscanway.com) has cooking courses in Italy, while Cuisine International (214-373-1161 or www.cuisineinternational.com)
  represents 18 cooking schools in Brazil, England, France, Portugal, and the United States.

For More Help

Travel and Learn, by Evelyn Kaye (Blue Panda) covers hundreds of
learning vacations, many designed specifically for women.

Travel Smart (800-FARE-OFF or www.TravelSmartnewsletter.com)
is a 27-year-old monthly consumer newsletter that specializes in
telling its readers how to travel better for less, with a focus on appealing destinations around the world.

Bottom Line

You'll discover that getting out, meeting new people, and seeing new
places quickly leads to a more enriched life, one that is both emotionally and physically enhanced. As George Bernard Shaw said,
"Travel is one way of lengthening life."

Chapter Eighteen

GETTING MARRIED AGAIN

There is more of good nature than of good sense at the bottom of most marriages.

—HENRY DAVID THOREAU

You know it happens. You saw it with your best friend, your colleague, or maybe your own mother or father. But you never thought it would happen to you—meeting someone new with whom you want to live. Yet it has, and a new chapter in your life is about to begin.

Before you rush to the altar, let's talk "good sense" and go over some of the financial details you need to consider. I don't want you to let good sense get in the way of your joy; on the other hand, I don't want joy to get in the way of protecting yourself and your children financially.

Because each person moves into a relationship with their own unique set of financial baggage, their own view of the lifestyle they want, and their own established saving and spending habits, it can take considerable time before even the most romantic couple strikes the right balance when it comes to dollars and sense. But thinking about how you'll share your property, money, and expenses ahead of time will make the transition easier and more successful. Resist insisting upon duplicating the money management styles you and your deceased husband used. This is a different person. So are you. A new era often calls for new approaches.

Before the Bells

As you're planning your big day, don't overlook the less romantic but equally important side of tying the knot—the financial paperwork: Make certain you do the following:

- Get insurance for your engagement and wedding rings. You can add a rider to your homeowner's or renter's policy. If you are having a large wedding and will be receiving many presents, they too should be covered.

- Tell your boss. Make an appointment to speak with your benefits officer or, if you work for a small company, your office manager. Let him or her know the date of your wedding, the name of your spouse, his Social Security number, and, if you're moving, your new address and phone number.

- Review your benefits. If both of you are working and insured through your employers, go over your health and dental coverage very carefully. If one plan is far superior, drop the poorer one and add that person's name to the better plan.

  If one of you is not covered at work or is a consultant or freelancer, that person should be added to the insured spouse's plan.

  Caution: Ask your benefits officer when you can make such changes. With some companies, changes must be made during a certain time frame, known as "open enrollment." You don't want to miss this narrow window of opportunity. And, at the same time, ask what the dollar amount of the new or revised contributions will be.

- Decide on your name. In order to change some ID papers, such as your Social Security card and, in some states, your driver's license, you'll need to present a certified copy of your marriage certificate. (You should receive this paper several weeks after the ceremony.) If you decide to change your name, check with the clerk of the court regarding specific regulations. The person officiating at your ceremony—a justice of the peace, judge, minister, priest, or rabbi—should also be aware of local procedures.

If you and your husband both want to change your names, say to a hyphenated version, the same procedures apply.

Notification of any name (and address) changes should be sent to all of these government agencies that apply: the Social Security Administration, the IRS, state and municipal taxing authorities, your local Registrar of Voters, the U.S. Passport Office, the Veterans Administration, Department of Motor Vehicles, and your local post office.

Others you should inform include your doctors, insurance companies, lawyer, accountant, bank, brokerage firm, library, credit card issuers, and telephone and utility companies. And you can also decide to change your name after the ceremony!

Prenuptial Agreements

It's impossible to say whether or not you should have a *prenuptial agreement*. It is possible to say you should consider one and consult a lawyer licensed to practice in the state where you and your husband-to-be will be living.

A prenuptial agreement is a legal contract signed before your marriage that spells out who will pay what expenses and how all of your assets will be divided in case of divorce or death. It gives both of you control over what you want to happen and it supersedes both inheritance and right of election laws.

Having your new husband limit or waive claims on your property will also help protect the rights of your children from your previous marriage. In fact, one of the key advantages of a prenup is that you can arrange for your children to inherit all of your assets or that portion you have specifically set aside for them.

Prenups are generally a good idea if:

- You own a business or are in a partnership.

- You have significant assets, such as real estate, trust funds, a brokerage account, and/or a high *net worth*.

- You have more money than your fiancé. The rule of thumb is twice as much, but this is an individual call.

- You have children from a previous marriage. This agreement makes sure that the assets you want to pass to your children will do so rather than to your new husband.

- You will be supporting your new spouse through school, especially professional graduate school.

- You have ongoing financial responsibilities for your parents or other family member.

- You will be coming into a sizable inheritance.

MAKING AN AIRTIGHT AGREEMENT

In order to make certain your prenup will stand up in case of divorce or a legal suit by a disgruntled husband or members of his family, it must airtight. That means:

- Each of you should be represented by your own lawyer. Do not share legal counsel. If you or your fiancé cannot afford a separate lawyer, the other should offer to pay for both lawyers.

- Both of you must sign the agreement willingly. If it can be proved that either person was coerced to sign, the agreement could be tossed out of court.

- The agreement cannot be signed at the last minute. Since a prenup requires disclosure of assets plus at least one legal discussion and/or negotiation, it cannot be done a day or two before the wedding.

- Both parties must reveal all details about their financial assets—salary, investments, real estate, income-producing property, bank and brokerage accounts, and debts. Hiding any asset or debt more often than not makes the agreement null and void. This process of disclosure will enable you to find out if your husband-to-be has debts you know nothing about. It is far better to hear about them now rather than when you return from the honeymoon.

- Assets, such as jewelry, antiques, artwork, collectibles, and real estate, should be appraised by an independent professional, not by you.

Finally, I recommend that you have a videotape made of both of you signing the agreement so you have a record.

SOME TYPICAL ASSET DISTRIBUTION OPTIONS

These are the four most common options for how assets can be handled during marriage:

1. Your premarital assets, including income and appreciation, remain 100% separate.

2. Your premarital assets remain separate, but all income on those assets is shared, either equally or by some other formula.

3. Your assets and his assets are pooled once you are married.

4. A percentage of your income and his income is shared; all else is kept separate.

OTHER ITEMS TO INCLUDE

Additional issues that are often dealt with in a prenup include where you'll live—your house, his house, or a new house—the purchase of long-term health insurance for one or both of you, an updating of both your wills, how you will share living expenses, and how you will handle the care and support of his children and aging parents and the care and support of your children and your parents.

TIMING

If you do decide to go ahead with an agreement, don't wait until the last minute. It typically takes three weeks to a month to work out all the details. You want to have the signed document in place long *before* you start writing out checks for the caterer and organist.

BOTTOM LINE

Widows who do not want to risk losing the assets they've accumulated over the years generally find prenups easier to arrange than young women getting married for the first time. However, if one of you is much wealthier than the other, the person with the smaller net worth may feel uncomfortable and may worry that their new spouse doesn't trust them. Your lawyers should be able to explain that this agreement will protect and comfort *both* of you.

After the Bells

- Update your will. As soon as you return from your honeymoon and write your thank you letters, set aside time to update important papers. Begin by revising your wills to include one another. You don't want the state to determine who will receive your worldly possessions. If you would like to take care of this before the wedding, you could add to your existing will something like, "If at the time of my death, I am married to Joe Smith, he is to inherit the following assets . . ."

- Set up his, her, and our accounts. Here's what I found works well for most second marriages, but you can make your own modifications as needed. Each of you maintains a separate checking account to pay for individual things, such as clothes, transportation to and from work, presents for each other, lunch or dinner out with friends, your health club membership, and school tuition or college loans. It should also be used to handle premarital debts and business expenses.

Then, have a joint checking account, earmarked to pay for all of the things you do together: paying the rent or mortgage, buying groceries, paying utilities, having a shared car, or going on vacations. There is no one-size-fits-all solution for how much each of you should contribute to joint savings and expenses. If both of you earn approximately the same amount, you may decide to split expenses 50/50.

If one of you earns much more than the other, you have to realize that this situation could lead to a subtle but definite feeling that the one with the larger income has more control. Instead of the 50/50 division, each of you could contribute a percentage of what you earn (or a percentage of your income) to your joint savings. This resolves the stickiness of dollar amounts, especially if one of you has a much fatter bank account.

You could also pool your money into a joint account and then withdraw what each needs for his or her individual accounts. Or, put each person's income into his or her account and together decide how much (or what percentages) each should transfer into a joint account for joint living expenses.

I definitely do not recommend pooling all of your money at the start of your new marriage. Wait until you've been together a while and are knowledgeable about each other's spending and saving patterns and personalities.

> $TIP: Skip having an ATM card attached to your joint checking account. People in a mad rush often withdraw money and forget to record it. This can lead to banking woes and ongoing personal arguments.

- Get a joint credit card. In addition to having one joint checking account, I recommend that you also have one joint credit card, designated for major "together" purchases, such as furniture, appliances, vacations, and general travel. Set a dollar limit above which you agree to check with each other before using this particular card. It could be $25, $250, or $2,500. This prevents either of you from bringing home an entire new sound system from the mall or a Harley from the dealer—unless you agree ahead of time.

And, vow to each other that you will faithfully pay off the balance, in full, each month and on time.

This, then, will be the only credit card that will show up on both of your credit reports.

Incidentally, both of you should get a copy of your individual credit card reports and share the information (see Chapter 7). It makes for an easier financial future if there are no surprises down the road. If it turns out that one of you has a poor credit report, find out why and work to clear it up as soon as possible.

- Change your beneficiaries. You will want to change the beneficiary designations on some or all of your investments and retirement accounts. If your husband had named his ex-wife as a beneficiary, that too should be updated. Among the items to review in this regard are:

  - EE savings bonds
  - Mutual funds
  - Brokerage accounts
  - Annuities
  - Life insurance
  - Trusts
  - IRAs, SEP IRAs, Keoghs
  - 401(k) or 403(b) plans
  - Stocks
  - Bonds

When a person dies, retirement savings plans, including traditional IRAs, the Roth IRAs, and 401(k) plans, go to the named beneficiary and not the heirs mentioned in a will. So, when you die, the person you named as beneficiary will receive the money in the plan, even if you left everything in your will to someone else.

- Visit your safe deposit box. If one of you has a box, arrange for the other to have access by signing a special document in the presence of a banking official. Know where the box and keys are located. If you don't have a box, rent one—for your marriage certificate, prenup agreement, copies of your new wills, and other key documents.

- Make adjustments. You may want to change your tax with-holdings and increase your contributions to retirement plans.

- Follow the two rules of sensibility. For every couple—whether gay or heterosexual, legally joined or not, or on their first or fifth marriage—there are two rules for a financially successful life: talking and sharing.

Until your remarriage, you were in many ways living as a single, basically making your own decisions, spending and sav-ing as you decided. If you wanted to use your savings for a week at a spa, no one said no way. If you were squirreling away every penny, it was your call. If you were trading stocks, fine. The same was probably also true for your new husband. But now that you're living under the same roof, you can no longer call all the shots—only some of them.

Make it a plan to regularly discuss money matters—per-haps once a month. This need not be a difficult discussion, provided you think of it as a business meeting. At your initial meeting, write down:

- How much each of you earns
- How much each of you has in savings and investments
- What each of you owns—house, car, motorcycle, timeshare, boat
- How much each of you has in outstanding debts

Then work out a budget based on your income and expenses (see Chapter 6) and periodically review how you're doing.

Neither of you should wind up doing all of the bill paying, tax preparation, and other money-related paperwork. Rotate these tasks on a semiannual or quarterly basis. Not only will this relieve the drudge work, but both of you will be informed and up to date. Then, if one of you is off climbing Mt. Everest or away on assignment or even ill, the other will be completely prepared to handle all your financial matters with ease.

Children and Remarriage

If either you or your new husband came into this marriage with children, you must address the issue of their expenses and inheritances. If large amounts of money are involved (or if you wind up arguing about who pays for what), consult a financial planner or your accountant or lawyer. Most remarried couples find it best to keep separate accounts for their own children's expenses. Over time, depending upon the relationship, how much money each of you has, and the ages of the children, you may decide to alter your initial arrangement. At the beginning, however, the natural parent is often the one footing most if not all of the child-related bills.

WHO GETS WHAT?

As we discussed in Chapter 2, the legal manner in which property is owned defines who will receive it upon the owner's death. If it is held jointly, it automatically goes to the surviving partner. If it is owned as tenants in common, then you can leave your portion to whomever you like, including your children. This is also true, of course, for property held in your name only.

This is all pretty easy to understand unless you live in one of the nine community property states. If you do, check with your attorney. Nearly all property acquired by you or your husband during the marriage in Arizona, California, Idaho, Louisiana, Nevada, New Mexico, Texas, Washington, and Wisconsin is said to be the "property of the marriage." That means when one of you dies, the surviving spouse inherits his or her half—almost always—regardless of whose name it is registered to.

Ask your lawyer if you should title the assets that you and your husband own together as tenants in common or tenants by the entirety. Or, if a postnuptial agreement can circumvent community property laws.

An exception: Property that you owned before marriage or acquired after you were married as a gift or as part of an inheritance is regarded as separate property in community property states. In other words, it is 100% yours.

SETTING UP A TRUST

Your attorney or accountant may recommend setting up a _trust_ to ensure that your property will go to the person you want it to go to.

A favorite with remarried couples is the _Qualified Terminable Interest Property (QTIP)_ trust. It not only postpones payment of estate taxes but, if one of you dies, all of the income generated by the trust goes to the surviving spouse for life. The surviving spouse, with the co-trustee's approval, usually can tap into the principal if it is needed to maintain his or her standard of living.

When the surviving spouse dies, whatever remains in the trust is passed on to the named beneficiaries. If you name your children from your first marriage as beneficiaries, then the assets will go to them upon your husband's death.

If your husband were to remarry, this type of trust also protects the interests of your children.

For More Help

About Getting Remarried, Life Advice (800-MET-LIFE or www. metlife.com)

Nolo's Pocket Guide to Family Law, by Robin Leonard and Stephen Elias (Nolo Press, 2000) is written by two attorneys.

Nolo's Everyday Law Book, by Shae Irving (Nolo Press, 1999) has a detailed chapter on prenuptial agreements.

Bottom Line

Marriage the second time around is different. You and your husband bring to it a past history. Keep in mind the words of Kahil Gibran:

> *Let there be spaces in your togetherness*
> *And let the winds of the heavens dance between you.*

GLOSSARY

Adjusted gross income (AGI): A tax-related figure arrived at by adding up all your income for the year to get your gross income and then subtracting adjustments. Adjustments include contributions to your qualified retirement accounts, alimony payments, qualified moving expenses, student loan interest, medical savings account deductions, and, if you're self-employed, half the self-employment tax. Once all these adjustments have been subtracted, you have your AGI.

All-risk insurance coverage: A type of property insurance that covers any and every loss, unless the loss is caused by an "excluded peril" that is specifically listed in the policy. (See **Peril**.)

Annuity: Annuities are like an insurance policy in reverse; you give the life insurance company a sum of money, which is invested, and the company in turn pays the holder of the annuity (the annuitant) a regular income, usually monthly, for a specific period of time—a number of years or for life. Annuities typically begin payments upon retirement, although an immediate annuity starts right away. A fixed annuity pays a guaranteed rate; a variable annuity produces returns that are tied to the performance of the market. *Note:* Your money grows without taxation until withdrawn.

Asset: A property or investment, including money, stocks, mutual funds, real estate, equipment, or anything else, that has monetary value that could be realized if sold.

Beneficiary: A person named in your will who will receive a stated asset or assets when you die. In the case of a life insurance policy or a pension plan, the beneficiary will receive your benefits. *Note:* You need to name a beneficiary for each type of account or policy.

Bill of lading: A contract between you and a moving company that determines your rights if anything goes wrong. It must include the name and address of the carrier, points of origin and destination, maximum dollar amount required to receive delivery, and type of insurance coverage.

Bonded: Refers to a worker (contractor, electrician, plumber, and so on) who has a type of insurance that guarantees he/she will meet his/her obligations. Failure to do so results in the payment of compensation by the bonding company.

Buy-sell agreement: A legal document that provides for the smooth succession of a business when certain events take place. It spells out how a co-owner, heir, or other person will buy interest in the business should the owner retire, become disabled, or die.

Cash value life insurance: A type of insurance in which a portion of the premium is used to provide death benefits for your beneficiary and the rest is invested in a savings-type account. Also called *"permanent* insurance" and "whole-life insurance." *Note:* In most cases, you can borrow the cash value of the policy at low interest rates.

Charge card: A card that requires you to pay your balance in full each billing period. It has no credit line or interest charges. *Note:* You are much less likely to run up huge bills if you know you must pay 100% of your charges on a monthly basis.

Claim: An official document requesting compensation or benefits from an insurance company. Claims are filed when there's an accident, fire, flood, or other type of damage.

COBRA: The federal legislation requiring health insurers and large employers to continue to offer health insurance, at the employee's expense, for 18 months after coverage is ended, typically when an employee is fired, laid off, put on part-time or leaves voluntarily. Coverage is extended to 36 weeks for widows and their dependent children.

Codicil: An addition made to an existing will. It can be merely an amendment or it can revoke a portion of the will.

Community property state: A state in which all earnings during marriage and all property acquired with those earnings are regarded as property owned jointly by the couple. At divorce, community property is divided in half between the spouses. A spouse who contributed separate money to an item essentially bought with community funds may be entitled to reimbursement for that contribution.

Compound interest: The amount earned on the original principal plus the accumulated interest. With interest on interest plus interest on principal, an investment grows more quickly.

Condominium: In a condominium, you own your own unit and a share of everything else. You essentially buy your living quarters from the walls inward. The outer structure and the grounds are collectively owned by the condominium association.

Co-op: A co-operative building is owned collectively by its residents. You, in turn, then own a share of the entire building. Co-ops are structured as corporations with each resident owning a portion of the total stock; the amount of stock owned depends on the size and value of the unit.

Copayments: The partial payment of a medical expense, emergency room service, or a prescription drug required by an individual who is enrolled in a group health insurance plan. For example, a copayment for a visit to a doctor's office might be $15. The payment is said to be "out of your own pocket."

Credit bureaus: Companies that gather information about your credit history—for example, how promptly you pay your bills—and then sell it to banks, mortgage lenders, credit card companies, department stores, insurance companies, landlords, and some employees. Credit bureaus obtain most of this information from creditors but they also search court records for lawsuits, judgments, and bankruptcy filings. *Note:* They do not make decisions about granting credit.

Credit report: Compiled by a credit bureau, a report that includes the names of your creditors, type and number of each account, when each account was opened, your payment history for the previous 24 to 26 months, your credit limit, and your current balances. It also shows if an account has been turned over to a collection agency or is in dispute.

Credit union: A co-operative or nonprofit association of people who pool together their savings and then lend money to one another. By law, they must have a common bond, which may consist in working together for the same employer; belonging to the same church, synagogue, or government agency; or even living in the same neighborhood. *Note:* Because overhead costs are low, credit unions give savers and borrowers better rates and terms than commercial banks and institutions.

Custodian: A financial institution that holds in custody someone else's assets—cash, securities, or virtually anything of value. The custodian is responsible for the safekeeping of these investments, including an IRA.

Custodian account: An account controlled by a custodian rather than the owner of the assets. These accounts, typically at a bank, brokerage firm, or mutual fund company, are often used for minors or others unable to handle their own assets.

Debit card: A plastic card issued by a bank that can be used to buy goods and services or to get cash. When you pay with a debit card, the money is automatically deducted from your checking account. *Note:* Many merchants accept ATM cards as debit cards. The advantage: you pay immediately rather than running up interest charges on a credit card bill.

Deductible: The amount of loss paid for by the holder of an insurance policy. It can be either a specific dollar amount or a percentage of the claim. For example, if your deductible is $500 and you have $800 worth of damage, the insurance company will cover $300 and you'll pay $500 out of pocket. *Note:* The bigger the deductible, the lower the premium you'll be charged for the same coverage.

Deduction: An expense you may subtract from your income that lowers your taxable income. Examples include mortgage interest, property taxes, and many retirement account contributions.

Depreciation: A special tax deduction given for the general wear and tear on rental real estate. It also applies to writing off the cost of business assets, such as cars, computers, and cell phones. Each type of property is depreciated over a certain number of years.

Down payment: The part of the purchase price for a piece of property that the buyer pays up front and in cash. It is not financed by a mortgage. *Note:* The larger the down payment, the better the deal you'll get on your mortgage. The best mortgage terms generally require a down payment of at least 20% of the purchase price.

Employee stock option: An option that allows an employee to purchase shares of the employer's stock at a predetermined price. Generally, no tax is due on any gain until the time of sale, if the sale date is at least one year after the date on which the option was granted.

Employee stock purchase plan: A plan that allows you to buy your company's stock at a discount. The discount is not taxed until you sell your shares.

Equity: The difference between the market value of your home and what you owe on your mortgage. If your house is worth $100,000 and your outstanding mortgage is $40,000, your equity is $60,000.

Estate: The total assets or property owned by a person at a specific time, usually upon his death. The value is arrived at by subtracting loans and liabilities from your assets. Estates worth over a certain dollar amount are taxable at the state and federal level.

Executor: A person (or institution) named in a will who is responsible for settling a deceased person's estate according to the instructions in the will.

401(k) plan: A type of retirement savings plan offered by many for-profit companies to their employees. Your contributions are exempt from federal and state income taxes until you withdraw the money, usually upon retirement. *Note:* Many companies match their employees' contributions.

403 (b) plan: A type of retirement savings plan that is very similar to a 401(k) plan, but designed for the employees of nonprofit organizations.

457 plan: A type of retirement savings plan that is similar to a 401(k) plan, but designed for state and local employees (firefighters, policemen, municipal employees) and for upper management employees of 501(c) tax-exempt organizations, such as hospitals, unions, and trade associations.

Fixed expenses: Those household expenses that cannot be changed (or changed very much), such as rent, mortgage payments, and utilities. (See **variable expenses.**)

Floater: Attached to a homeowner's policy, a floater insures moveable property, covering losses wherever they may occur. A floater is most often used to cover expensive jewelry, furs, and musical instruments, computers, printers, and fax machines.

Foreclose: The process by which you lose your home because you were unable to make the required mortgage payments. Each state has its own rules governing the process.

Grace period: The time period provided in most loan agreements and insurance policies during which default or cancellation will not occur even though your payment is past due.

High-risk insurance pool: A state plan that provides insurance for those who cannot purchase it in the open market from insurance companies due to high-risk factors. These plans cover health and auto insurance.

Home equity loan: This is basically a second mortgage in which you borrow against the equity in your house. It is often used to pay off high-interest consumer debt or to tap into when needed for shorter-term needs, such as to remodel your house or pay college tuition. *Note:* The interest payments are tax deductible.

In street name: When securities are held in the name of the broker, not the client, the broker sends the client dividend checks, annual reports, and proxies.

Insurance: Various types of products sold by insurance companies to individuals and businesses that will reimburse them in the event of loss. The insurer profits by investing the premiums it receives from it customers. Insurance can cover business risks, automobiles, boats, homes, worker's compensation, and health. Life insurance guarantees payments to the beneficiaries when the insured person dies. *Note:* Insurance transfers risk from individual to a larger group, which is better able to afford to pay for losses.

Interest: Money paid for the use of money.

Interest rate: What lenders charge you to use their money.

Intestate: This means you have died without setting up a will. State law then determines what happens to your worldly possessions and assets as well as who will care for your minor children.

IRA: An Individual Retirement Account. This can be set up by anyone who has employment income or alimony. Contributions may or may not be tax deductible, depending upon IRS regulations. *Note:* The amount you can contribute has gone up to $3,000 a year.

IRA rollover: A technique that allows employees to avoid taxes by transferring lump-sum payments from a 401(k) or other retirement plan into a rollover IRA.

Joint tenancy with right of survivorship (JTWRS): This is ownership of property in which two or more people each own an equal share. They may give away or sell their share without the permission of the other owner(s). In the event of death, an owner's share is divided equally among the surviving co-owners. (See **Tenancy by the entirety** and **Tenancy in common.**)

Key-man insurance: Insurance on the life or health of a key employee whose services are essential to the continuing success of a business and whose death or disability could cause the firm substantial financial loss.

Liquid: Investments, such as money market funds or bank certificates of deposit, that can easily and quickly be converted into cash.

Medigap insurance: A policy that supplements federal insurance benefits, particularly those covered under Medicare.

Net worth: The total value of cash, property, and investments after deducting all outstanding bills and amounts owed.

Open enrollment: A specific time period each year when employees or retirees may enroll in a health or dental care plan, change plans, or add eligible dependents.

Pension plan: Also known as a defined benefit plan. Pensions are offered by some employers as a benefit for their employees. They typically pay you a monthly retirement income based on the number of years you worked for the company.

Peril: A specific risk or cause of loss covered by an insurance policy, such as fire, windstorm, flood, or theft. A named peril policy covers the policyholder only for the risks named in the policy, in contrast with an "all-risk" policy, which covers all causes of loss except those specifically excluded.

Points: The prepaid interest that a borrower pays to get a mortgage. This interest is often tax deductible.

Preexisting condition: Any physical or mental condition that exists prior to the date when health insurance coverage begins. Most disability policies and individual health plans exclude benefits for any illness or injury for which a person received medical treatment or consultation within a specified time before being covered under the plan.

Premiums: The payments, usually made on a regular periodic basis, that a policyholder makes to an insurance company in order to own his or her policy.

Prenuptial agreement: An agreement made before a couple marries concerning certain aspects of their relationship. It may cover their responsibilities (who will pay the mortgage) and, in the event of divorce, how property will be divided and whether alimony will be paid.

Principal: The amount you borrow for a loan. If you borrowed $50,000, then your principal is $50,000.

Probate: The formal process of proving the authenticity of the deceased person's will and confirming the assignment of the executor.

Profit sharing plan: A type of employer Keogh plan where the annual contribution made to the plan for employees may vary from year to year as a percentage of the employee's profits or each individual employee's salary.

Qualified Terminable Interest Property (QTIP): A marital-deduction trust in which the surviving spouse receives income from the trust's assets for life but the trust's principal is left to someone else, usually children. It limits the surviving spouse's access to and control of the property in the trust. (See **Trust.**)

Refinancing: Refi, as it's called today, involves taking out a new mortgage loan (usually at a lower rate) to pay off an existing mortgage (usually at a higher rate).

Reverse mortgage: A mortgage that enables senior citizens who are low on cash to remain in their homes by tapping into the home's equity without having to sell or move.

Rider: An amendment or attachment to an insurance policy that modifies the policy. It can expand or restrict its benefits or exclude certain conditions from coverage.

Second mortgage: A traditional, additional (or second) mortgage, usually with a fixed rate loan for a fixed amount of money, with a fixed payoff date. (See **Home equity loan.**)

Secured card: A type of credit card that is secured by money deposited with the bank. You may be able to charge up to half or nearly all the amount the bank is holding. Fees and rates can be exceptionally high. *Note:* Use if you cannot get credit any other way.

Settling the estate: This refers to the process of collecting all the assets of the deceased, paying claims, handling the administrative details, and distributing the remaining assets. It entails transferring the title to the property in the deceased person's estate to the heirs.

Sinking funds: Assets set aside to protect a business or asset.

Tenancy by the entirety: A type of ownership limited to married couples in which each spouse owns an equal share of the asset but neither may sell or give away an interest without the other's permission. If one spouse dies, the deceased's share automatically passes to the surviving spouse.

Tenancy in common: A type of ownership for two or more people in which, when one of the owners dies, his/her share passes to heirs if a will is left or to the estate if there is no will. It does not go to the other co-owners.

Term life insurance: This covers the insured for a certain period of time, usually for the "term" specified in the policy. It pays a benefit to the designated person only when the insured dies within that specified time, which can be 1, 5, 10, or even 20 years. *Note:* Term policies are renewable but the premiums increase dramatically with age.

Totten trust: A type of "in trust for" account, usually at a bank. You have control of the account during your lifetime but upon your death, the account goes to a named beneficiary. *Note:* Totten trusts avoid probate. (See **Trust.**)

Transfer on death account: A legal agreement through which, upon the death of the person who drew up the agreement, ownership of the named assets will pass to the named beneficiary. *Note:* Transfer on death accounts bypass probate.

Treasuries: An IOU-type investment issued by the federal government that individuals and institutions may buy. All treasuries pay interest that is free from state but not federal income taxes. Treasury bills come due (mature) within a year. Treasury notes mature in one to ten years, whereas treasury bonds mature in ten years or more. *Note:* Along with EE savings bonds, treasuries are among the safest of investments because they are backed by the U.S. government.

Trust: A legal arrangement that passes ownership of your assets to someone else. A trust actually holds money or property for someone else and is managed by a trustee. The trustee can be an individual or an institution. (See **Totten trust.**)

Variable expenses: Those household expenses that can be changed—either increased or decreased—such as restaurant dining, travel, entertainment, and luxury items. (See **Fixed expenses.**)

Vested benefits: The nonforfeitable dollar amount in a retirement plan that belongs to the employee, even if he/she leaves the job. An employee typically becomes vested after five years. Until you are vested, you cannot take your employer's contributions and earnings with you if you leave your job, get fired, or retire. You can keep all of your contributions and earnings.

Will: A legal document that spells out your wishes regarding your assets and care of your minor children that must be followed when you die. It determines the distribution of your property to others.

INDEX

Handyman Connection, 169
Handymen, 169–170
Hart, Moss, 167
Health care proxy, 133–134, 142–143, 152
Health insurance. *See* Insurance
Help! I Am a Parent of College-Bound Children, 224
Home improvement loans, 171–172
Home Insurance Basics, 106
Home Made Money: A Consumer Guide To Reverse Mortgages, 166
Homeowner's insurance. *See* Insurance
House and home
  household inventory, 104
  moving, 174–205
  remodeling, 167
  remodeling loans, 171–172
  renting for income, 156
  swapping, 241–242
How to Administer an Estate: A Step-by-Step Guide for Families and Friends, 21
How to Live with Your Remodeling Project, 172
How Work Affects Your Social Security Benefits, 231
Humphrey, Herbert H., 34

Individual Retirement Accounts. *See* IRAs
Institute of Financial Planners, 113
Intestate, 16
Insurance. *See also* COBRA
  auto, 96–102
  claims, filing for deceased persons, 34
  disability, 75–76
  flood, 103–104
  health, 39, 72–76
  homeowner's, 102–106
  keeping policies, 152
  key-man, 47
  liability, 106
  life, 90–95
  long-term care, 85–88
  major companies, 40
  Medicare/Medigap
  ratings of companies, 87–88
Interior Arrangement & Design Association, 170
Interior decorator, 170
Interior designer, 170
International Funeral Association, 8
IRAs
  rollovers, 41
  Roth, 223

Job hunting. *See* Work
Johnson, Lyndon Baines, 27
Joint tenancy with right of survivorship, 20

Kaufman, George S., 167
Keller, Helen, 205
Kelley Blue Book, 101, 202
Key-man insurance, 47
Kipling, Rudyard, 236
Kroc, Ray, 152

Lawyer. *See* Financial advisors
Letter of instruction, 4–6, 151
Life insurance, 90–95
  beneficiary of, 34–39
  cash value, 92–94
  filing claims, 34–36
  major companies, 40
  payments, 27
  term insurance, 91–92
  universal life, 94
  variable life, 94
Lincoln, Abraham, 3
Living will, 135, 144–145, 152
Long-Term Care Planning: A Dollar and Sense Guide, 88

Marriage certificate, 10, 152
Martindale-Hubbell Law Directory, 118
Medicaid, 83–85
Medicaid: A Brief Summary, 85
Medicare, 76–80
  fraud, 81
Medicare Handbook, 82
Medigap insurance, 80–81
Military discharge papers, 11
Mortgages
  foreclosure, 160
  home equity loan, 160–164
  refinancing, 157–160
  reverse, 165–167
Moving, 174–205
  back home, 209–210
  garage sales, 177–178
  moving companies, 189–194
  moving insurance, 194–196
  resolving disputes, 199–200
  selling vs renting, 175

National Academy of Elder Law Attorneys, 84
National Archives Records Administration, 32